Trade, Aid, or What?

TRADE, AID, OR WHAT?

A Report Based Upon A Conference on

INTERNATIONAL ECONOMIC POLICY

At The Merrill Center for Economics
Summer — 1953

BY

WILLARD L. THORP

Director of The Merrill Center for Economics
and
Professor of Economics at Amherst College

1954

THE JOHNS HOPKINS PRESS

The publication of this book was made possible by a generous contribution from the Merrill Foundation for Advancement of Financial Knowledge.

To

Charles E. Merrill
a practical dreamer

With the grateful appreciation
of all who have shared their ideas and their pleasures
at The Merrill Center for Economics

Preface

No BOOK can reproduce the excitement of a lively discussion. When such discussions have continued for eight weeks, the most that can be done is to try to recapture as many of the considerations, complications, and evaluations as possible. There is little room for the countless illustrations or the spontaneous bits of humor which gave life to the hours spent around the conference table. But such prolonged discussions were bound to give new contours and perspectives to many problems and these are worth reporting.

The Merrill Center for Economics held its opening exercises on June 28, 1953. The discussion began the following morning and continued vigorously for eight weeks. The central topic was " Trade, Aid, or What? " and there were forty-five conferees, selected on the basis of their ability to contribute to the discussions. In addition, fourteen specially invited guest speakers led discussions on particular subjects.[1] The sessions were divided roughly into three main categories dealing respectively, if not respectfully, with commercial policy, exchange policy, and foreign investment policy. The number of conferees participating in the discussion of each of these areas ranged from twenty-one to twenty-seven.

No agenda was prepared in advance and the first task of each group was to settle on the problems within its broad area which it wished to discuss. No report was planned and no effort was made to force a consensus. It was a conference of experts for the purpose of discovering their agreements and exploring their disagreements, based on the assumption that the project would sufficiently justify itself through the reflection of such an intensive interchange in the subsequent activity of the conferees as teachers, writers, advisors, business men and public servants.

[1] For a list of conferees and guest speakers, see page xi.

Certain generalizations can be made as the result of the summer's experience. The first is that many of the problems are far more complicated than the participants individually had believed them to be. The experts represented various points of view and different backgrounds. When they pooled their knowledge and experience, the number of considerations which needed to be taken into account in making policy decisions inevitably increased. Discussion does not necessarily mean controversy. It may be rather the building up of a composite picture of the problem, to which work of art a number of individuals are able to supply bits and pieces. It also became clear that there are many areas where it may be possible to agree on causes and effects but to disagree on the magnitudes involved or speed of reaction to be expected (the effect of a lowering of the United States tariff; the point at which birth rates will begin to fall; the capital-absorbing capacity of underdeveloped countries).

Secondly, it was demonstrated over and over again that problems and policies in the international economic field are inextricably interrelated with each other and with domestic policies. It was impossible, except for certain theoretical analyses, to confine any problem to an intellectual enclave, for it soon broke out in some direction or other, either to raise new problems in areas already explored or to necessitate moving into territory presumably to be reached later on the tentative agenda. The effects of economic behavior in a particular situation may be circular, radiating, cumulative, compensatory, or counteracting, but never sterile. The simple point is that any economic problem has wide ramifications.

Thirdly, the discussions demonstrated conclusively that people frequently do not disagree as much as they believe they do. The exploration of what had originally appeared to be disagreements often disclosed that there was no real disagreement at all but either a difference in emphasis to be given to the several elements in the problem or a misunderstanding of each other's position. Sometimes it was merely a difference in the use of terms. (One conferee assembled twenty-nine different definitions of " balance of payments.") In other cases, differences in experience had led to different approaches to a problem and an exchange of information led to a common analysis.

Finally, there was one set of propositions on which there was complete agreement, that international economic policies are of vital importance, that they can strengthen or undermine a nation's foreign relations, and that the economic capabilities and effective use of resources are greater for countries working together than for the total of them taken separately. Nor were these problems regarded as abstract and unreal. In the discussions, they were alive and moving and disturbing. There was a sense of urgency—that in this world of little distances and unbelievably high explosives, both literally and figuratively, it is of tremendous importance to the future to think and act wisely today.

Against this background of eight weeks of discussion, this report has been prepared. No recording was made of the sessions, although the conferees in turn undertook to prepare rough summary notes. Nor would it be a service to the reader to give a verbatim report. After all, the discussions lasted nearly two hundred hours. Like all vigorous discussions, they not always took the most orderly form and some issues were discussed many different times, often from quite different angles. Since the conferees were selected because of their knowledge and experience with the problems under discussion, it was frequently possible to use verbal shorthand and references around the table rather than to elaborate a point in detail.

A complete report also would have to cover many points of limited general interest but of great technical interest to some of the participants. Furthermore, since the conferees lived together, discussions frequently continued at the dining room table, in the gardens, or at the bathing beach, and an accurate account of the eight weeks would have to cover these side explorations as well. For all these reasons, this report is not and cannot be a replica of the discussions. It is rather an attempt

to put together in a somewhat more orderly form some of the
more significant ideas which emerged during the eight weeks.
The report must be thought of as outlining problems and
indicating considerations rather than as endeavoring to put
forward any specific program. It must be clearly understood
that it cannot be regarded as either an agreed consensus or the
reflection of all the views of any one conferee (including the
scribe). It is simply a report based upon the discussions.

To present such a report at all is something of an experiment. People do not spend much time discussing matters on
which they are in agreement, so there is bound to be an
emphasis on the new, the unusual, and the controversial which
may obscure the degree of basic agreement. Futhermore, it is
easy to record conflicting considerations but impossible to
note all qualifications, and frequently a discussion ended with
individuals recognizing that the final conclusion depended
upon the particular circumstances under which the problem
arose. This may give an impression of indecisiveness which
was not present in the minds of the participants. Nor can the
scribe, being a person of opinions, be sure whether his own
biases are showing, or whether he has leaned over backwards
beyond the point of balance.

In preparing this volume, the Director of the Merrill Center
is indebted to all the conferees who shared not only their
ideas but also the burden of keeping rough notes of the discussions. Even more, must he express his appreciation for the
special assistance in organizing and preparing the report, gen-
erously given by Alexander Cairncross, Isador Lubin, Fritz
Machlup, Austin Robinson, Walter Salant, Joseph J. Spengler,
Robert Triffin, and Raymond Vernon. However, the Director
alone must take the final responsibility for these pages, sadly
recognizing that no man or group of men could possibly reflect
adequately on paper the unique experience of the eight weeks
together at The Orchard in Southampton.

CONFEREES, 1953

Thomas C. Blaisdell, Jr.
William A. Brown, Jr.
Alexander K. Cairncross
Walter Chudson
Arnold P. Collery
Jack C. Corbett
Richard H. Demuth
Read P. Dunn, Jr.
George A. Elliott
Grover W. Ensley
Frank W. Fetter
Isaiah Frank
Hugh Gaitskell
Kermit Gordon
Wytze Gorter
Arnold Harberger
Samuel P. Hayes, Jr.
René Higonnet
Folke Hilgerdt
Francis T. Juster
Svend Laursen
Jack M. Letiche
Isador Lubin

Ansel Luxford
Fritz Machlup
Robert Marjolin
Raymond F. Mikesell
Chandler Morse
James R. Nelson
H. Austin Peck
Howard Piquet
Austin Robinson
Jerome Rothenberg
Sir John Saint
Walter Salant
Robert Schaetzel
Frank A. Southard, Jr.
Joseph J. Spengler
Leroy Stinebower
Stanley Surrey
Willard L. Thorp
Robert Triffin
Raymond Vernon
Westmore Willcox
Eric Wyndham-White

VISITING SPEAKERS, 1953

Benjamin Haggott Beckhart
Eugene Black
Charles W. Cole
Dag Hammarskjöld
Averell Harriman
Don D. Humphrey
Milton Katz

Max Lerner
Gaganvihari Lallubhai Mehta
Frank W. Notestein
Franz Pick
Morris Rosenthal
William S. Swingle
John Williams

Table of Contents

List of Abbreviations

BIS   —Bank of International Settlements

ECA   —Economic Cooperation Administration

ECE   —Economic Commission for Europe

EPU   —European Payments Union

ERP   —European Recovery Program

FOA   —Foreign Operations Administration

GATT—General Agreement on Tariffs and Trade

IBRD —The International Bank for Reconstruction and
          Development

IFC   —International Finance Corporation

IMF   —International Monetary Fund

ITO   —International Trade Organization

MSA   —Mutual Security Administration

NATO—North Atlantic Treaty Organization

OEEC —Organization for European Economic Cooperation

TCA   —Technical Cooperation Administration

UK   —United Kingdom

Trade, Aid, or What?

CHAPTER I

Problems and Objectives

THE ECONOMIC DISORDER

WHEN the war ended in 1945, both production and trade had fallen to low levels over large parts of the world. In spite of many difficulties, industrial production recovered rapidly in most countries. The resumption of international trade was slower and by 1947 the volume of the total imports of the principal countries of western Europe still remained 15 per cent below the 1938 level and the volume of their exports was 33 per cent below 1938. During the years 1947 to 1951, there was a remarkable improvement, stimulated and facilitated by the European Recovery Program, but representing a real expansion in both production and trade far beyond the actual dimensions of that program. By 1951, the volume of imports of the same group of countries was 15 per cent above the level of 1938 and the volume of exports was 51 per cent above it. During the same period, the volume of exports from the United States had risen to more than double that of prewar, while the volume of imports had advanced more slowly to about 50 per cent above the 1936–38 level.

The postwar increases in production and trade varied greatly from country to country both in extent and in timing. However, it is fair to say that progress was spectacular despite all the difficulties of war destruction and disorganization. In 1951, abnormal price gyrations, inventory accumulation, and stepping up of military programs induced by the Korean War

3

caused a temporary slowdown in many countries, but the advance was resumed on a broad front in 1953.

The problems faced by these countries were not merely those of re-establishing the old pattern, for that would not have been good enough. Difficulties in international economic life were already apparent before the war. To these troublesome inheritances had to be added the loss of overseas income and the increase in overseas liabilities, the reduction in other sources of invisible income, the substantial shift in the terms of trade, and the changed position of the United States in the world picture. The currency systems were plagued by different degrees of inflation, overvaluation, and inconvertibility, and by a general inadequacy of reserve levels. There were many obstacles to trade, including changed trade patterns related to the iron curtain. It is clear that there were and still are serious problems which require solution before the economies of the free world (the world free of Soviet domination) are fully restored to health and comfortably on the road to further expansion.

In addition to the problems which cluster around the processes of trade and payments, there is a second focal point which is likewise of major importance—international investment. The insistent desire of many countries to begin or to accelerate the process of economic development raises many problems made more difficult by the changes which have taken place in the international capital market. The foreign investment experience of the nineteenth century was related to a different world and the record of the first half of this century has not provided a basis for enthusiastic foreign investment along the old lines. What contribution can foreign capital make to economic development, under what circumstances can it be expected to become available, what sort of institutions are required?—these are among the questions for which answers must be found.

The problems of trade and payments and of foreign investment are by no means unrelated. Progress in any one area is likely to facilitate progress in others. However, for purposes of analysis, problems must be somewhat abstracted from each other.

The Trade and Payments Problem

In what sense can there be said to be a trade and payments problem today? It is obvious that over a period of time no country can acquire more imports of goods and services than it is able to get by purchase from its earnings, by credit, by gifts, or by payment from its foreign assets or monetary reserves. If a country possesses neither means of payment nor credit, it will perforce achieve a balance by sheer inability to acquire imports. Like any system of double-entry bookkeeping, it must always be in balance. What then is the problem?

What seems to be essentially at issue is the ability to finance a volume of imports of goods and services that is believed to be necessary or desirable if the economy in question is to continue to operate in certain ways and to achieve certain present and future living standards. What is feared is that the inability to acquire such imports will endanger the actual working of the economy or reduce living standards to a physically or politically dangerous level. To be more specific, most of the countries of the world have found it difficult to earn by their own exports of goods and services, or to borrow on their future expectations, enough dollars to buy the quantities of goods and services that they wish to import from North America and at the same time to satisfy their needs at home and the demands of other markets to which they have to export. Others are able to achieve an over-all balance but cannot find ways of off-setting their deficits with some areas against their surpluses with other areas.

What is in question for many countries is the future extent of their foreign earnings and the degree to which they will be applicable at the points where the desired goods can be purchased. For short periods, a country may support its foreign payments by drawing on reserves and by short period borrowing. To achieve a long-term adjustment, domestic changes in production and consumption may be necessary. Nor can any country disregard developments in other countries. On the one hand are the prospects that its earnings can be enlarged by

increased prosperity in other countries or by greater opportunities to sell exports in particular markets or by improved
processes of multilateral settlement. On the other is the possibility that even present earnings may be threatened by an
adverse shift in the terms of trade or by a reduction in foreign
demand or by some increase in international tension. Within a
framework of such uncertainties, each country must construct
its economic foreign policy.

Nor, as will appear again and again, can economic foreign
policy be considered apart from domestic policy and practice
The war period was so disturbing to the various economies
that no government could leave the allocation of resources and
finished goods to the usual market-place mechanisms. A large
part of the wartime controls has been dismantled, but the
trend of the twentieth century towards more and more government planning and responsibility has not been reversed. Domestic policies directed to maintaining full employment, to
supporting agricultural income, or to encouraging investment
all have their implications with respect to international economic relations, and to the nature of the adjustments which
can be made to improve the trade and payments picture.

The Long-Term Structural Adjustment

Unfortunately, it is not always clear in a given situation of
disequilibrium whether there is a basic source of difficulty or
whether the causes are temporary and accidental and require
no basic correction. However, it is certain that present payments problems have not arrived overnight. International
economic relations were already under strain in the thirties.
The prewar difficulties with currencies and the increase of
trade restrictions were largely related to the depression, but
there were long-term shifts taking place which still underlie
the situation today.

The great phenomenon of this century has been the rise
in the importance of the United States in world trade. While
both her imports and exports remain much smaller in proportion to national income than those of most other countries, the

sheer extent of United States economic activity has made it both the world's largest importer and largest exporter. Until 1913, the growth of the United States share in world trade was more than offset by the growth in trade, so that European countries continued to expand their exports and their imports. After the 1920's, world trade ceased to grow at anything approaching the pre-1913 rate. Europe had increasing difficulty in selling its exports in competition with the United States and Japan. European countries found themselves doing a smaller proportion of a smaller export trade, while at the same time being confronted by increasing difficulties in maintaining the levels of imports required by their growing populations.

These problems were already becoming serious by the 1930's. The United Kingdom ran deficits on current account. Germany experimented with multiple currency arrangements. Even then, attempts were made to dispense with imports from North America, partly by encouragements and protection to home industries and agriculture, partly by preferences given to softer currency sources of supply. The difficulties of the United Kingdom were reflected in the difficulties of western Europe, which used to earn dollars from a surplus with the United Kingdom.

The growth of United States exports and the relative decline of those of Europe were associated with, and probably in large part due to, the more rapid economic advance of the United States. A less rapidly advancing country is likely to find itself handicapped in competition with a more rapidly advancing country which may be able to lower prices while maintaining or even increasing wages and earnings. It may seem plausible that the less rapidly advancing country may conceivably be driven into deflationary policies discouraging technical improvements and investment and finally degenerating into an economic backwater. Whatever the truth of this last hypothesis (and most economists would deny it, saying that when comparative advantages change, labor and capital adjustments will operate to maintain external equilibrium), there is little doubt that trade is attracted to the country with technical leadership and that in many industries the leadership had passed from the European countries which enjoyed it in the early phases of the Industrial Revolution to the United States. Thus, quite apart from the effect of wars, the countries of Europe which have lived and maintained their dense populations by the export of manufactures (a high proportion being in textiles whose production was rapidly expanding in other countries), would have been forced to modify their structures and possibly to reduce their dependence on foreign trade to accord with the realities of the world in which they lived.

During the 1930's these problems did not force themselves on the world or create the strains which have emerged since the war, principally because the terms of trade became for a period exceptionally favorable to the export of manufactures. The volume of United Kingdom imports which cost 100 units of exports in 1931–38 would have cost about 145 units in 1906–10. These favorable terms of trade have been attributed in part to more rapid progress in agriculture and other primary production than in industry. But they were undoubtedly in larger part the result of the deep depression of the 1930's when, as is usually true of depressions, prices of primary products fell much more than did those of finished goods. Furthermore, during this period, the great preoccupation of most countries was the maintenance of employment within their borders. If their policies in pursuit of this objective led to an external balance achieved by an outflow of gold, this was unfortunate but hopefully temporary. Thus, at the outbreak of war, the world was by no means fully adjusted to the hard realities of the contemporary situation.

Nor have more recent developments entirely eased these problems. The war and postwar periods saw tremendous capital investments, innovations, and technological advance in the United States. In many other areas outside of Europe and North America, new manufacturing industries have developed rapidly. The prewar exchange between western Europe and eastern Europe of manufactured goods for foodstuffs has dwindled. For western Europe, the payments problem seems to lead either to reduced living standards or the achievement of some new pattern of expanding world trade.

At the present time, most of the countries of the world face this same difficulty of adjustment, a reflection of their demand for certain foreign goods and services available only in certain markets, set against certain short-term inelasticities, structural maladjustments, and bilateral channelings which limit their foreign earnings possibilities. At any moment of time a country has a given pattern of productive capacity and applicable manpower; this can only be modified significantly over a period long enough to permit new investments and the necessary transfers of workers. Many of the new investments in underdeveloped countries (e. g., power and irrigation) are reflected only slowly in their foreign economic relations. In a relatively free economy, where investment is undertaken only in response to demand and transfers of workers depend on the relative rewards and employment prospects in different occupations, it may be a matter of some years before its structure becomes fully adjusted to a substantially changed economic environment.

This process of structural adjustment has been proceeding rapidly since the war. The capacities of European exporting industries are being developed to increase their foreign earning power. European domestic sources of supply are being built up where possible to reduce their dependence on imports. Alternative sources of imports in soft currency areas are in process of creation. New sources of dollar-earning primary products are being expanded in parts of the world where European countries can hope to acquire the resultant dollars by their exports. The changing pattern of resources is now much more fitted to the needs of the postwar situation than that of 1947 when the United Kingdom made its abortive attempt to restore convertibility of sterling.

But it is not yet complete. It can be expected that in the course of the next few years all these changes will contribute to easing the problems both of European countries and those of the rest of the free world. Meanwhile it remains difficult for many countries to pay for current demands for foreign goods and services with current earnings.

SOURCES OF DIFFICULTY

The problem of structural adjustment has been complicated by the wide variations and uncertainties of the terms of trade, that is, the relationship between the price of exports and the price of imports. For countries which live largely by the export of manufactures, the severe and sudden upward movement in the price of raw materials which followed the outbreak of the Korean War implied a sudden and unexpected necessity either to make heavy reductions of imports or large increases of exports. Countries which exported raw materials found themselves with a large increase in their foreign exchange resources. The more recent trend in relative prices between prices of raw materials and of manufactured goods has again greatly changed the picture for many countries. It is impossible in a world of violently changing relative prices to judge quickly and with any certainty whether or not changed circumstances justify or require an expansion of exporting capacity, and what ultimate pattern of resources is needed to meet the longer-run circumstances of the postwar world.

To these major difficulties have been added a number of contributing factors, at least some of which could have been remedied within the powers of individual governments. In some cases, inadequate taxation or insufficient savings to cover the requirements of current capital formation, with consequent inflationary pressures, have led to increased demand in the labor market, to a spiral of rising wages and rising prices, and to the diversion of manpower from export to home production. This inflationary process in turn has led to the overvaluation of currencies at existing exchange rates and to serious handicaps for exporters.

In other cases, the inadequacy of currency reserves has meant that temporary and short-period disturbances, which in prewar conditions would have been met by drawing on reserves, have precipitated an exchange crisis or a drastic curtailment of imports with severe repercussions on other countries.

In other cases, the shortage of gold or dollar reserves, the recurrence of exchange crises, and the possibility, or indeed the likelihood, of devaluation have resulted in heavy speculation in a currency, so that no remedial measures within the power of the government or central bank concerned could be powerful enough to prevent its breakdown.

Of recent great importance has been the effect of rearmament. The rise of defense expenditures from the order of 6 per cent of the gross national product to over 10 per cent in a number of instances, when added to the needs to replace capital destroyed or worn out during the war, to modernize industries, and to maintain tolerable consumption standards, has created further inflationary pressures. At the same time it has diverted from export a large volume of the engineering capacity which is a main source of export earnings in the principal European countries. Even though much of the required military equipment is being provided by the United States, the burden of building and maintaining military strength on other countries has been heavy.

Another element of difficulty has been the uncertain participation in the world economy of countries under Soviet domination. In large part, trade with these countries used to take the form of the exchange of manufactured products, particularly capital goods, for agricultural commodities. However, the emphasis in such countries on industrialization and self-sufficiency has restricted such exchanges, while the separation of Eastern Germany and the absorption of Czechoslovakia have tended to direct their potential export activity towards the East. In addition to these limiting factors is the policy on the part of the free world to restrict trade on items which might contribute to military potential. This necessary orientation of trade has not affected all countries equally but has been a major complication for some which traditionally have traded actively with the countries now behind the iron curtain.

This brief summary of some of the factors which have con-

tributed to the trade and payments problem (when properly
defined) suggests that it reflects long-term and short-term
causes, that it stems from economic and noneconomic sources,
and that it is widespread in its incidence. It will be considered
from many different angles in subsequent pages.

The Demand for Economic Development

The trade and payments problem takes on a somewhat
different aspect when it is viewed in the light, not so much of
meeting current bills, as of the prospects of economic improvement. Here the problem centers less about imports and exports of goods and services than about the flow of capital, of
capital goods, and of future payments. Concern over economic
development arises because of the existence of wide disparities
of per capita income in different parts of the world with resultant problems of poverty and malnutrition which cause not only
great human suffering but also grave dangers of political unrest
and even revolution. For political, economic, social, and hu-
manitarian reasons, the richer countries of the free world cannot afford to be completely unconcerned about the welfare of
the poorer countries.

Underlying these great differences of wealth and poverty are
great differences not only in mobilized resources but also in
the rate of social and economic change. It is not many genera-
tions since the countries of western Europe had standards of
life little above those of some of the poorer countries of Asia
today. Within the memory of many now living, Japan has
advanced from a pre-industrial society even less developed than
present-day India or China to a progressive and developing
society, and Turkey seems to be following the same pattern.

The nineteenth century was one in which rapid economic
development took place in Europe and North America. Many
elements contributed to the speed and extent of the expansion.
The frontier and new resources, the substantial redistribution
of manpower, and the accumulation of capital, all made possible
the rapid exploitation of new scientific and organizational ideas.

The spirit of enterprise functioning within economies where there was little regulation or restriction by governments created certain social problems which later were dealt with by government action, but it also provided the drive for rapid expansion.

In the nineteenth century, economic development like most economic activity did not take place according to plan or as the result of much governmental encouragement (except perhaps the development of transportation). There was little consciousness on the part of the underdeveloped that they were underdeveloped. Today the picture is quite different. In many important areas, nationalism has gone through a political phase leading to political independence and now has turned to the economic, focussing on development. Knowledge of differences in the level of living has greatly increased. Communism and capitalism are compared as routes to economic advancement. And politicians, having made promises, are judged by the progress which is made.

Many difficult problems are created by this demand for development. In countries where incomes are already miserably low, can consumption be depressed still further to make capital formation possible? What are the requirements for development in addition to capital? Can foreign assistance be ingested in the light of the anti-foreign spirit which underlies political nationalism? Can foreign capital be attracted anyway?

In connection with the last question, one new development in this field during the last decade is the much greater part played by governments and their institutions in providing capital assistance to other countries. Technical assistance also is being offered by governments on an organized basis as never before. The United Nations agencies are new elements in the picture. But even assuming some increase over present levels of foreign assistance, what are the prospects for substantial economic advancement of these areas? How much must they do themselves and how much can the richer, technically more advanced and advancing, countries help them to establish a cumulative process of growth? How does one break out of one social and economic pattern into another? If the best and most

appropriate technical knowledge and sufficient supplies of capital to acquire the first installments of equipment from abroad
are provided, can it be hoped that, out of rising national incomes and increasing margins above the barest means of subsistence, they will presently be able to find the savings, the
enterprise, and the know-how to carry on the cumulative
process, as happened in western Europe and the areas of European settlement and more recently in Japan and in the Soviet
Union?

The future of these economies is clearly of major importance to the world. It is conceivable that these areas will
become much more important in the world economy both as
suppliers of mineral and agricultural products and as expanding
markets. New forms of triangular exchange might emerge
which would aid in solving the problems of Europe. The
problems involved are much more difficult to analyze than those
in adjusting trade relations. Here, a social and economic revolution is required; and knowledge about cause and effect in
such circumstances is limited indeed.

THE MAIN OBJECTIVES

The problems of trade and payments and of economic development have both affected international economic relationships in the same way. Both have increased the desire for more
goods from the dollar area. These demands, accentuated by
exceptional requirements for capital equipment both to repair
wartime destruction and depreciation and to expand industrial
capacity and by shortages or delayed delivery dates of supplies
from non-dollar sources, have led to what has often been called
a "dollar shortage." To this phrase a variety of meanings can
be attached. The less justifiable of such meanings would imply
that the United States has been at fault in not matching the
desire of others to buy with limitless supplies of dollars. To
any such claim there are obvious answers. However, the sim-
plest is that in practice, in every year since 1948, the United
States has made dollars available to the rest of the world on a

scale which has permitted such countries in aggregate to increase rather than reduce their reserves.

The present balance between the dollar area and the rest of the world is achieved with the assistance not only of United States aid which in various forms puts goods at the disposal of other countries without requiring payment, but also by means of a variety of limitations placed by the other countries on expenditure in the dollar area. Through such devices as national trade and exchange restrictions as well as group action such as the sterling area dollar pool, scarce dollars are rationed and dollar payments limited to the volume that has been acquired by trade and aid. Parenthetically, these many restrictions run often not only to dollars but to various other currencies as well.

It is the desire of most of the countries that are engaged in rationing dollars in this way to move increasingly towards greater freedom and a relaxation of these impediments along with a reduction in the volume of aid. But this can only be done without a curtailment in trade if it coincides with an increase of dollar earnings, though some of the pressure on the dollar would disappear if there were freer trade within the non-dollar area. If balance is secured by further devaluations and other measures which operate chiefly to diminish the world demand for dollar exports, then greater freedom and fewer obstacles to export will not bring in their train any actual increase in trade. And it is not a matter of indifference whether a balance is struck at a low level of trade or at a high level of trade; the best international division of labor would imply the desirability of a higher level of trade than is immediately in prospect.

The current situation must be appraised in the wider context of the whole international division of labor of the free world and of the extent to which goods might profitably be exchanged in accord with specialization in those activities in which each nation has a comparative advantage. This involves problems of the structure and dimensions of world trade, of the restoring of trade consequent both upon long-term and short-term trends, and of the future relations of the United States economy to the world economy and to the economies of the free nations in particular. The separate problems of trade, of foreign exchanges, of capital flow, and of the internal use of resources by countries are essentially no more than different aspects of the single problem of the best and most profitable use of the world's resources and the part that international trade and exchange should play in facilitating the best use of those resources.

What, then, should be the main objectives of the economic policies of the countries of the free world today? About the main essentials there would almost certainly be a large measure of unanimity. Probably every country, whatever its political institutions and climate, its national aspirations, or its state of development or stagnation, would subscribe to the desirability of a steadily expanding national income, a reasonably equitable distribution of that income, an economic structure and deployment of resources which will make the best use of the latter, a relatively stable course of production and employment, and a reasonable opportunity to exchange its exports in international trade for the products which for some reason or other it is handicapped in producing for itself.

The complications of policy-making arise at the second stage. In the first place, the economic objectives themselves are not wholly independent of each other. The objective of a steadily advancing economy implies a judgment between the relative desirabilities of steadiness and of advance. The objective of a reasonably equitable distribution of the nation's income implies a judgment between the desirabilities of a pattern of incomes which will yield the greatest total of satisfaction to consumers and the pattern which will best create incentives and stimulate savings and capital investment. And these conflicts of objectives keep on appearing throughout the whole field of policy-making.

As between objectives, and particularly as between the objectives of progress achieved at the expense of painful repercussions and stability purchased at the price of slower progress, not only individuals but also whole nations will put the main emphasis on one objective or the other. Not infrequently a nation may fail to recognize that one of these objectives is secured at the expense of another. Or it may believe, as in the field of international trade, that it can use a weapon against others without the same weapon being turned against itself.

But more specifically in the international economic field what can be said about objectives? In considering the specific problems and situations dealt with in later chapters, it may be helpful to keep at least three such objectives in mind:

(a) *Large and expanding opportunities for trade.*

The place of trade in the efficient use of the world's resources has already been noted. When world trade is thrown out of shape, as it was by the depression and the war, there is always a danger that the process of trade will be restored only after a cumulative contraction in which one country after another seeks to restrict its trade and reduce its dependence on foreign markets. It would have been possible in the postwar world to allow this degenerative process to operate unchecked; and there can be little doubt that but for loans and grants from North America, something like a collapse in the whole structure of trade would have occurred. Even now, strong arguments are put forth in many countries for developing what may seem to be a relatively stable home market rather than exposing the economy to the instability of world markets. Although the alternative is often a false one and the sacrifice in real income may be considerable, many individuals continue to regard international trade with some distrust.

Yet there will be general agreement that efforts to restore balance at a low level of trade are painful not only to the countries caught out of balance but also to their neighbors. If national incomes and international trade are both expanding, it will be easier for the pattern of resources to be pulled into place comparatively gently instead of being pushed about brusquely and unwillingly. Structural change and economic development can take place more easily. One of the first objects of commercial and financial policy must be to seek to achieve a higher level of trade and to try to ensure that this high level can be maintained without extended aid.

This does not mean that every sort of international trade is "good." For example, it was probably not very helpful to anybody when, some years ago, the Swedes exported typewriters and printing machines to England and the British exported typewriters and printing machines to Sweden; not that they preferred the imported ones to their own but the control authorities of both countries were so anxious to promote exports that they prohibited domestic sales of these exportable products. But this is merely an example of bad controls and not an argument against international trade.

(b) *More multilateral trade.*

The recovery of trade after the war was accompanied in the early stages by a great network of bilateral agreements. Where neither party had the means of settlement in gold or convertible currencies, these agreements allowed trade to proceed where it might otherwise have come to a standstill. But they were an expedient, and in many ways an inconvenient expedient. From the economic point of view they frequently obliged countries to buy from high cost sources of supply and to accept goods that ranked low in their scale of preferences. From the political point of view, they tended to expose countries having little choice of markets or sources of supply to the dictation of countries in a strong bargaining position, much as the countries of eastern Europe found themselves in the thirties geared more and more closely to the German war economy with less and less advantage. Bilateral agreements also inevitably involved discrimination against third countries, often of a quite arbitrary kind, and frequently provoked resentment and even retaliation.

Bilateral trade agreements are still important; and a high proportion of international trade is, and has always been, bilateral in the quite different sense that the balance remaining for settlement between any two countries is usually only a small fraction of the total volume of business between them. The restoration of multilateral trade is clearly bound up with progress towards currency convertibility. The basic argument for multilateralism and convertibility is that they would permit trade to flow about the world in accordance with demand and supply rather than under a bilateral process which comes close to barter. Multilateralism leads to a much higher level of trade and a much higher degree of international specialization. The problem of payments would be not that of each country with each other country, but of each country with all other countries, under which circumstance bilateral deficits and surpluses could balance each other out.

(c) *More stable trade.*

A high level of trade eases the process of adjustment for individual countries; multilateral trade allows countries to derive the maximum advantage from the use of scarce resources situated abroad; both require a measure of stability if these results are to follow. But trade fluctuates both in volume and value and for some countries, particularly those engaged in primary production, the fluctuations are large and frequent. Quite small fluctuations in the demand of final consumers, after being transmitted through several stages of processing with all the attendant magnifying changes in inventories, are likely to emerge on a far larger scale at the raw materials end of the chain.

Nor is it only the primary producers who are subject to trade fluctuations. Other countries, themselves involved in trade with the primary producers, are affected. Moreover, a change in the level of activity in the leading industrial countries, and particularly in the United States which accounts for half the industrial output of the world, is felt at once all over the world and can produce quite startling effects on trade balances. The objective of stability is important for any country; it is also important internationally.

These objectives have been stated in terms of trade, but they also have meaning in terms of capital movement. The same logic and economic purposes which urge expanded opportunities for the flow of goods would seem to call for an increased and more stable flow of capital.

The degree of importance which should be given to these international objectives, which seldom dovetail neatly into domestic objectives, is of course related to the significance of international economic relationships to the economy involved. It can be questioned as to how important they are, *per se*, as objectives for the United States. To be sure, the United States needs certain raw materials from abroad, although its present exports are far more than sufficient to pay for them. More important, many of its industries are built on a scale assuming an export market, but there are alternative domestic uses for resources and adjustments, though painful, could be made if necessary. (It may be that a greater degree of stability in export markets could be more important than reaching higher peaks.) Even if all United States foreign investments, public and private, were to default, the economy would hardly feel the blow. In terms of an economy operating with a gross national product aproaching $400 billions per year, the economic gains to the United States from further trade expansion are relatively small. If the primary objective of foreign economic policy is to get richer, the game for the United States may not be worth the candle.

But the more appealing and defensible objective, justified on quite different grounds, is to expand the real income and the stability of other economies. To them, their foreign economic relationships are of much greater importance, often a major determinant of the level of their economic existence as well as its future. There is no necessary antagonism between those who emphasize the expanding trade objective on the part of the United States and those who act out of concern for the economies of other countries. These two objectives point in the same general direction. However, it may make considerable difference in the specific approach to specific policy issues and in the devices which are used. The economic objectives become important as part of much broader objectives of foreign policy.

The Problems of Policy-Making

Economic objectives cannot therefore be pursued in isolation. In creating his working model for the study of a theoretical world, an economist may assume that countries are pursuing the objective of that international deployment of resources which yields the greatest real income to the world as a whole in a period of sustained peace, and in which every nation is prepared and anxious to specialize in those activities— and only those—for which it has the greatest comparative advantage. The practical policy-maker cannot forget that war as well as peace is a possibility, that he must have in mind the possible effects of given policies on war potentials, or that he must remember the vulnerability of a wholly specialized and undiversified economy, whose population may be stimulated in one generation and find itself workless in the next.

These problems of judging between and reconciling conflicting ends of policy are further complicated by the added problems of judging between alternative means of policy. It not infrequently happens that, for the reasons just outlined, the solution of a given economic problem which is most desirable on theoretical grounds turns out in practice to be unacceptable. Even if it be agreed that the world of perfect competition among small units unfettered by restrictions on trade will give the best deployment of resources, there may be little or no prospect that in any reasonable period of time this ideal world can be brought into existence or kept in existence. In such circumstances, the practical policy-maker in the economic field must decide for himself whether he believes it best to persist in attempts to create the best of all possible worlds, or whether it may not be better to accept a second best alternative which though inferior to the theoretical best is yet better than the existing state of affairs. He must decide which of the possible worlds is the best available world.

This means that the abstract objective and even the means to be used will be affected greatly in practice by international, domestic, and bureaucratic political implications. In fact, as a practical matter, the proposed " ideal " solution to a problem is constantly watered down and modified not merely by the political " experts " but also by the economic " experts " who are seeking to anticipate political objections. It therefore is not unlikely that on at least some occasions, the economist may make more concessions to " political reality " than would the political experts themselves, if they were given a full understanding of the problem and the technical solution thereto. When economists are charged with being impractical, as they sometimes are, it may be that they are merely functioning within the limitations of their expert knowledge.

The differences of economists over matters of policy-making spring comparatively seldom from fundamental disagreements over analysis. Such disagreements arise from time to time on the frontiers of the subject and are hotly disputed, but as a rule a sufficient measure of agreement for working purposes emerges comparatively quickly. The differences in regard to policy-making spring principally from two sources: first, from differences in judgment about the relative importance of two incompatible objectives of policy—stability or progress, equality or incentive, saving or spending, a narrow definition or a wide definition of the group whom policy should benefit; second, from differences of judgment about the efficacy of different instruments of policy—how controls can or cannot be made to work, the virtues of fluctuating as against fixed exchange rates, and so on.

These are all matters about which it is both natural and proper that any group of individuals should differ. Sometimes such differences can be narrowed or even eliminated by fuller knowledge, such as is provided by intensive study of the actual working of institutions. But other differences are rooted deep in the values that all of us as individuals attach to particular ends of life and ways of life. We can learn to appreciate other views, but no amount of exchange of views will or should wholly eliminate these differences.

CHAPTER II

Adjustment by Aid and Controls

THERE are a number of ways in which a "deficit" country can act to bring its international economic relations more nearly into balance. It may take certain "cushioning" measures: (a) it can draw on its foreign assets or reserves, if any; (b) it can finance foreign purchases by credits, if they can be arranged; (c) it can be helped by foreign aid. It may take certain "readjusting" measures: (d) it can change the rate of exchange, thus affecting both imports and exports; (e) it can shift domestic resources into export-producing and thus endeavor to increase its foreign earnings; and (f) it can place obstacles in the way of transactions which will draw on its limited supply of foreign exchange.

All these methods have been used by various countries during the postwar period. They are not mutually exclusive and can be used in various combinations. Of course, in an inconvertible world, a country in over-all balance may still have many bilateral problems. Certain of these same processes must be followed in regional or bilateral adjustment in cases where a country has a deficit with some areas even though it may have a surplus with others, unless the obvious multilateral clearing or exchange solution is available to it.

The first of these devices, the use of foreign assets and reserves, is of course limited by the amount of assets and reserves available. Large amounts of foreign assets were liquidated during the war and in the immediate postwar years. Reserves have taken the brunt of the onset of trouble in a

number of postwar crises, notably those of the sterling area
in 1947, 1949, and 1951, and in the case of several Latin
American countries, but obviously this cannot provide a long-
run solution for a persisting deficit.

Credits (item b) have also played an important part in
postwar adjustment. Many bilateral agreements have included
short-term credit features and the same is found in the European Payments Union machinery. However, these are thought
of as " swing " adjusters, to take care of temporary imbalances.
The prewar type of commercial bank credit has played no important part but government credits (particularly if one
stretches the term to include such operations as drawing on
sterling balances) have been important, though some of them
are perilously close to belonging in the category of aid.

As to the fourth device (item d), there have been more
than one hundred devaluations, usually intended to correct
an imbalance in trade but frequently falling short of achieving
the result. In fact, these currency adjustments have usually
served to offset past inflation and thus their effectiveness turns
in large part on whether or not the inflationary forces have been
brought under control. In several cases, exchange rates have
been allowed some flexibility, but there has been real resistance
to the use of such techniques since they can lead to costly
worsening of the terms of trade and may require unpopular
domestic policies to prevent offsetting domestic adjustments in
wages and prices.

The fifth of these devices (item e), the expansion of foreign
earnings, has been the goal of most countries, and along this
line real progress has been made. That this type of adjustment
has not moved forward even faster is in part a production
problem, but more often, a marketing problem. This may be
either the result of various difficulties in entering foreign markets or the fact that its products, particularly if they are raw
materials, may have such an inelastic demand that an increased
supply by lowering the price might even reduce the total
return. In addition, there is no doubt but that the necessary
emphasis on defense and the diversion to the production of

defense items of domestic resources which were or might have been used for export-producing, have interfered considerably with the expansion of exports by a number of countries.

None of the four adjusters discussed above, however, should be given short shrift. They have each been important and each will be discussed elsewhere in more detail. The point to be made here is that the remaining two approaches—the provision of aid (item c) and the curtailment of demand (item f)—have been the two last-ditch equilibrators in this period. These are, of course, not unrelated. Had there not been aid, the import programs of the various countries might have had to be even more curtailed, probably by much more than the amount of aid itself, for the aid undoubtedly contributed to their export programs. Had there been more aid, the restrictions curtailing demand would not have needed to be so great. As will be discussed below, these two adjusters have tendencies to persist and they need to be considered in general terms before looking at them in detail.

THE USE OF AID FOR BALANCING PAYMENTS

A considerable element in the postwar balances of payments is represented by aid in all its various forms. The greatest part of aid has been provided by the United States, but Canada has given her share, and other countries, particularly those responsible for overseas territories, have also made their contributions.

The official United States figures for " gross foreign aid " from the end of the war to the end of 1952 total $41.0 billions, and " net foreign aid " is reported as $37.6 billions. These are the summations of many different programs not including United States investments in the International Bank or the International Monetary Fund, nor private assistance or private investment abroad.

It is easy to argue endlessly over what items should appropriately be described as " aid." Should any distinction be made between grants and loans? And if loans are to be included, what about those with a clear American interest, such as one by the Export-Import Bank to an American firm to develop strategic materials abroad? The varied expenditures included in the total figures include such items as credits in connection with the disposal of war surplus, grants to the Philippines to meet war damage claims, the contribution of capital to EPU, and the shipping costs for goods sent abroad by private relief agencies.

The largest item in the program today is military assistance, and here there would be many (chiefly in Europe) who would question whether this expenditure should be regarded as aid at all. A joint program was developed in the North Atlantic Treaty Organization, based on the notion that there would be an effort to achieve " equitable burden-sharing." Some countries were to provide more bases than others, some more men than others, and some more equipment that others—all to be allocated as fairly as possible. The United States share in the burden is the maintenance of a certain number of divisions in Europe and the providing of a substantial part of the military equipment required. The NATO program is as much in the interest of the United States as of the other member countries. The appropriation is for Mutual Security Assistance, but to most people there is little distinction between this aid program and those which went before. Perhaps they are right, but if so, the conclusion might equally be that none of these expenditures should be called " aid."

It becomes even more difficult to determine how much of this so-called aid has operated to reduce so-called balance-of-payments deficits. Clearly, the United Nations Relief and Rehabilitation Administration aid provided relief goods which were greatly needed and so did the European Recovery Program. But when United States aid took the form of American tobacco to Germany displacing Greek and Turkish tobacco, the case is not so clear. And when aid is used to finance a project which might otherwise not be done at all, there would be no net gain in the payments situation. In general, if the aid had not been provided, the goods would not have moved from the United States. There would have been no deficit in payments but rather a deficiency in the supply of goods obtained as compared with those which the recipient countries felt were necessary to their economic recovery.

Aid has been valuable to the recipient countries in two fundamentally different ways: first, in enlarging their resources; second, in helping them to buy in the dollar area in circumstances of inability to obtain goods or to make multilateral transfers of surplus earnings from other areas.

In the early years after the war, the aid provided to Europe was important in both these respects. The absolute addition to resources was in few cases very large, but the additions were economically strategic, actually making operation possible where otherwise labor and capital might have been idle. The aid given to Europe was valuable principally in making available materials and foodstuffs without which severe unemployment and hardship were inescapable. It undoubtedly added far more to the national income than its own value.

With the great growth of European production since 1947, the need in Europe for aid for this purpose has largely disappeared. According to the estimates of the United Nations Economic Commission for Europe, the volume of production in the countries included in the Organization for European Economic Cooperation rose from about 76 per cent of the 1938 level in 1947 to 132 per cent of it in 1951. There are special problems concerning certain countries, especially Austria, Greece, and Turkey, but by and large the argument for aid in terms of lack of resources to maintain standards of living or to keep the economic machinery operating is now much less powerful than it was a few years ago.

The problem which remains is one of obtaining purchasing power which is usable in the dollar area. There are many who would argue that this problem is one of structural adjustment, that this takes time, that aid has provided this time, but that too much or too long a period of aid will reduce the pressure for the adjustment and postpone the point where balance is again achieved.

In some few cases, the rapid step-up in the defense effort of the last two or three years has revived the question of the adequacy of total resources. (Remember that the United Kingdom said in 1950 that she could get along without aid.) Quite apart from any possible problems of how equitably the burdens of defense are being shared, an issue on which there is a good deal of very natural disagreement, the added burden on some of the nations concerned would seem to have brought one or two of them dangerously near to the point where inflation cannot be controlled without major changes of policy. This is not to say that an adequate solution is to add a small fraction to the available resources through foreign aid. But it is obvious that in a sense it is true in such a case, as in all cases of inflation and overloading, that the inadequacy of resources to objectives is one aspect of the problem and that it would be somewhat easier of solution if the resources were larger.

This problem created by rearmament cannot be dismissed in terms of percentages and by noting what a minor fraction of resources is involved. Rearmament creates three special immediate difficulties. First is the fact that its demands rest particularly upon certain resources—the young men and the engineering industries. Since for Europe, much of its export trade comes from these same industries, the expansion of armament production has an immediately perverse effect upon the balance of payments. Second, since rearmament is a government undertaking, it requires a rechanneling of income into the public sector. With limited capacities to borrow, the result is to require increased taxes, a not always easy achievement, or to suffer inflation. Third, for various reasons much of the modern military equipment must come from the United States at a time when dollar earnings are inadequate for even normal commodities.

That so much progress has been made is the result of progress in adjusting to the problem by European countries and the rapid rise in the element of military aid in the United States program. Much of this aid has been in the form of military equipment. Except that it confuses the statistical picture of trade, this does not directly affect the balance-of-payments problem.

Certain other alleviating elements in the situation should be noted. The common effort has involved substantial United States financial participation in the expansion of defense installations in other countries. Also the stationing of United States troops abroad involves a dollar flow both for expenditures for maintenance and for local purchases by the soldiers. And the off-shore procurement program has made it possible for countries to receive dollars for military equipment which they have produced and turned over to other countries according to plan.

There is, of course, no way of forecasting how long these dollar flows will continue at their present levels. If they should be reduced, foreign dollar earnings will be affected accordingly. Furthermore, if building up defensive strength continues to be a major objective and if the American position at some future time should be one of wishing to have payment made for new military equipment, as well as placing on each country the burden of future maintenance and replacement, the effect on the balance of payments might be severe, sufficient even possibly to jeopardize the objective of the maintenance of an adequate defense.

THE USE OF AID FOR DEVELOPMENT

What has been said above about the growing sufficiency of European resources for the reasonable non-defense objectives of most European countries is by no means equally true of the poorer and less developed countries of the world. In those countries, resources appear to be inadequate to provide reasonable human standards and to permit capital formation sufficient to lift their standards as years go by.

The added resources that such countries require may be provided on a loan basis or in the form of grants. Chapter VIII will deal in more detail with this question. But some of the more general arguments can be outlined here, since they are relevant to the necessity for aid. If they are to succeed in generating a cumulative process of development, minimum amounts of capital are required for three main purposes: overhead capital investment in transport facilities, communications, power supplies, irrigation, and public utilities generally; social capital designed to raise standards of general and technical education, improve health services, and provide housing; industrial capital providing for the production of primary products, including food, and for expanding manufacturing and trade. For our purposes here, it is assumed that, even though they were fully mobilized, the savings of these countries are not sufficient to meet these requirements.

Part of this investment ought to be made on strictly commercial criteria. Where the political environment is favorable, much of it may come from direct private investment, although that will tend to concentrate in the industrial capital sector. Not all of the investment needs can be expected to be met from this source. Even by the strictest economic criteria, there is justification for more investment than complete dependence on private sources would afford. An improvement in the public utility services will pave the way for other investment and increase the return to it. Investment which cheapens sources of supply and makes the terms of trade more favorable may benefit an investing country to a greater extent than the returns to the individual investor. A developing and richer world will offer greater opportunities for specialization and trade in the future.

But even if there is a considerable increase of development on a loan basis, it is to be doubted whether such loans and direct equity investment together can provide the volume of funds which can be used advantageously and without waste. This doubt is reinforced when account is taken of the problems of servicing the debt. It is clearly desirable that a good deal of investment should take the form of improving education and other social services as well as that of improving public utilities. If loans are to be serviced, there must be an increase in productivity and in exporting or import-saving capacity over an appreciably shorter period than that in which long-term investment in education and health can reasonably be expected to yield dividends. Thus there is no doubt that the recognition that there is some scope and function for continued public aid is quite consistent with the view that certain aspects of development are best conducted on commercial criteria and where possible by private investment.

To an increasing degree, then, the justification of aid on the ground of inadequacy of resources is becoming confined to the poorer and underdeveloped countries. Most of the countries of Europe are anxious that it should be so. They almost unanimously prefer to pay their way rather than to accept what can be interpreted as charity. They are anxious to recover their sense of self-respect and independence which, however far from the intentions of the giver, seem somehow to be impaired by the receipt of aid. Thus on all these grounds, the narrowing and redefinition of the field of aid which has been taking place in the past few years is wholly appropriate.

The difficulty with pushing this argument to its logical and practical conclusions springs almost entirely from other important functions which the grants of aid have performed and which may still be needed. First is the function of contributing to the multilateral settlement of trade balances and the achievement of convertibility. In some cases, the more than bilateral effect of aid was not in the original plan—for example, the Anglo-American loan where the benefits went largely to other parts of the sterling area. But later aid programs, including offshore purchases, grants of conditional aid, and the providing of capital for EPU, all aimed not only at providing dollar-earning power, but of insuring at least one added step of non-United States trade.

A more difficult point is the relationship of aid to the building up of foreign reserves. In the case of the Chinese Nationalist government, there was no problem with respect to giving their currency cover; but when some European countries continued to receive aid and build up reserves at the same time, American policy was to cut back on their aid. And even in the early years of the Marshall Plan, the calculated balances of payments to be achieved did not include any strengthening of reserves. Yet this point is of some importance if convertibility has any real meaning as a goal. Reserves must be increased before most governments will dare take such a step.

But aid also has served other purposes, some of which have proved to be rather mixed blessings, politically and economically. It has helped many governments to achieve certain objectives which might have been difficult if they had depended upon domestic legislation, particularly if added taxes had been required. (Counterpart funds were of great value for this purpose.) It has opened the way for the United States government to participate in some aspects of planning and programming in other countries. And it has served to move large quantities of American goods. It should be noted that in the early postwar years and again in the months following the Korean aggression, much of this was done only by restricting American domestic demand, an angle of our assistance which is seldom appreciated. But foreign aid has helped to move agricultural commodities where production was so greatly expanded during the war years, and in the last Congressional appropriation special attention was given to the possible use of aid in moving agricultural surpluses.

The more we examine the notion of " aid," the more heterogeneous it appears to be, having served many different purposes in many different ways. Except that it is clear that goods going out of the United States are on the export side of the ledger and that dollars recorded as aid are on the opposite side of the accounting, it is not always clear as to how these two are related or what other elements in the balance of payments may be involved, either in the short run or ultimately. For example, it is perfectly possible that a little aid, by providing an economically strategic element, might lead to increased national income and an even greater demand for imports. Or it might be that aid in the form of military equipment would take young men away from the factory to man the new equipment and divert other resources which might be used in producing exportable goods, so the capacity to export would be reduced by aid. Or it might be that aid would increase export capacity and far more than pay for itself in the balance of payments. Or aid might be used to pay for items which would have been paid from other earnings, which in turn might be used for other purposes—servicing capital, for example.

Other elements, however, are clearer—that a program such as that of NATO can only be successful if the United States carries a large part of the economic burden; that any rapid progress in the form of economic development of underdeveloped areas will require aid (as the term is commonly used); and that aid is not without importance in the United States both in developing cooperative programs with other countries and in dealing with some problems of surpluses created by certain domestic programs.

THE RESTRICTION OF DEMAND

Even after aid had been taken into account, countries frequently found themselves still in difficulty, with the volume of purchases from countries with harder currencies than theirs draining away their reserves, building up commercial indebtedness, or putting tremendous pressure on the exchange rate. The final form of adjustment in the trade and payments equation has been for the government concerned to define and limit the effective demand by quota restrictions, exchange allocations, government purchase, or tax arrangements of one kind or another.

If all that were involved were the adjustment of international payments, restrictions would be fixed at a level such that foreign exchange expenditures would be balanced with foreign exchange receipts (unless some change in the reserve situation were also desired). This adjustment would take into account, of course, the amount of aid which was anticipated, if any. It is not necessary to be too skillful in estimating very far into the future, since restrictions would presumably be relaxed if foreign earnings plus aid increased, and tightened if foreign earnings plus aid were reduced. They would therefore act as a substitute for the nineteenth century adjustments working through gold movements, interest rates, and price level changes, effecting the final adjustment by controlling the volume of imports or the allocation of foreign exchange or both.

Once the notion of controls is accepted, it raises not only the question of the total impact desired to be achieved on the balance of payments (as well as other possible objectives), but also the shape and form of the impact. The restrictions can be used to discriminate between currencies, between countries, between industries, between products, and even between individual business men. Therefore not only the legislation and the regulations become important but also the actual practices. Depending upon the objective sought, the various devices which are available may be of varying utility. Thus tariffs are less useful in controlling trade in varying degrees according to country than exchange control, and quotas are more effective in discriminating among commodities than currency restrictions. In fact, there is no such thing as discrimination for the sake of discrimination, so that differential treatment may take many forms depending upon the purposes which it is meant to serve.

Even when controls are being employed for balance-of-payments reasons, they cannot help but affect the consumption and production pattern within the country. While the balance-of-payments justification is the only one which would receive general acceptance, controls are frequently defended as important instruments in making international economic life conform as much as possible to domestic purposes. A number of these arguments will be examined in the next chapter.

" Trade, not Aid "

That the international economic picture has greatly improved cannot be denied. Aid, other than the contribution of military goods, has been reduced from year to year and restrictions have not been appreciably increased, perhaps have even been slightly reduced. Economic aid at the end of 1953 was at the rate of about $2 billions per year. To be sure, the situation has some uncertain supports. The terms of trade have improved substantially in favor of western Europe but no one can say how permanent this may be. Another important and helpful factor has been the expansion of United States foreign operations since the Communist invasion of Korea, which has led to increased dollar payments abroad by the government for goods and services. These expenditures reached the rate of $2.5 billions per year in the last half of 1952 and as of the end of 1953 were running at an annual rate of about $3 billions. This has been an important factor in assisting certain other countries, particularly Japan, to earn dollars. It presumably is not a permanent element at the present level in future balance-of-payment expectations.

It might appear that the point has now been reached for most countries where, so long as purchases from the dollar area continue to be limited by exchange controls and quantitative restrictions, a balance, not considering defense, can be achieved without economic aid. It is certainly true that for several years many countries have preferred to build up their scanty gold and dollar reserves rather than use the whole of their receipts to enlarge their dollar imports. As the need to build reserves diminishes (an uncertain point), there may be, at present terms of trade, elbowroom for some further increase of dollar imports. As was indicated above, the main concern of many countries is to be able both to eliminate their dependence on aid and to relax their restrictions on United States products so as to be able to buy more in the dollar area.

However, the process of substituting trade for aid is by no means as simple as it looks on the face of it. Clearly, it does not imply that the adjustment to non-aid status will be made by reducing purchases from the United States. This would be merely " not aid." Rather it means the substitution of earned dollars for gift dollars. In Chapter V, we will discuss the penetrability of the American market, but for the purpose of this discussion, let us assume that such steps can and are taken so that the necessary expansion in dollar earnings is possible (disregarding the important element of military aid, of course) .

Additional resources in the country involved will now have to be devoted to earning dollars. This will be only an organizational problem if it has unemployed resources which can be put to this purpose. (However, one wonders why they were not used before for domestic purposes or for exports. Certainly, absence of aid will not make it easier, though perhaps more necessary.) If the country is already operating at capacity with full employment and wishes to substitute trade for aid, it clearly means that it must be prepared to make some sacrifices in domestic consumption or investment. The substitution of payment for gift will reduce the resources available for its own use. If the amount is small, it might be absorbed among all the other elements of fluctuation in any economy, but it will not be so easy in some cases, and quite impossible in others. Some countries can produce goods and services appropriate for the dollar market more easily than others. In any event, dollar earning will create an added strain and the justification would have to lie in necessity or national pride. From the planning point of view, there is one important gain—the amount of aid is outside the recipient's control and appears as an uncertain and limited amount, while trade means the opportunity to trade. Aid is apt to be a shrinking basis for imports, while the opportunity to trade may open the door to an expanding economic situation.

But a bilateral analysis by no means tells the whole story. If a country had earned surpluses with non-dollar areas, it might be able to shift exports from their present channels to dollar markets if they were less restricted. This might eliminate the hardship of any internal adjustment on its part and would shift the burden to a third country. The problem of the adjustment may thus be in part transferable, possibly increasing the need for aid in other areas.

This shift in incidence may happen also through price changes. If trade is substituted for aid, in the sense of increasing the United States market for certain imports, a short-term consequence (in some cases even a long-term consequence) may be to raise the price of these goods in the world market and

to turn the terms of trade against the countries which were
previously buying them. For example, if food products which
are bought by England from Australia, New Zealand, and
Denmark find a larger market in the United States, England
may have to pay higher prices for them and would suffer some
added reduction of the real standard of life or have more
difficulty in getting along without aid.

There is still a further complication in the fact that neither
aid nor trade is entirely controlled in its direction. Aid
to one country may in fact be flowing through that country to
a third country. And exports to the dollar area, so long as
barriers are reduced in the dollar area (the necessary assumption) and the most-favored-nation principle continues to be
applied, will not necessarily expand from the various countries
in accordance with the present aid programs. In fact, imports
into the United States would presumably have to increase considerably more than the aid, if it were to prevent added restrictions in some of the aid-receiving countries. To be sure, they
could compete with the United States for the additional dollars
earned by third countries, but most of the dollars in third
countries would probably be spent directly in the United States.
Furthermore, it could be that there would be an adverse movement of the terms of trade because a non-aid-receiving country
(Argentina) might sell more to the United States so that prices
for Argentine products would rise in an aid-receiving country
(United Kingdom), in which case the increase in trade might
actually increase the need for aid.

If it is possible for a country to increase its dollar earnings
to a degree equal to the dollars which it has been receiving as
aid and if the aid is then eliminated, this still does not " solve "
the payments problem in any basic sense. The balance will continue to be achieved by the use of trade or exchange controls
to reduce the effective demand for dollar goods. How much
the suppressed demand is, is impossible to say. Since the controls are set to define the amount of dollar goods to be admitted,
there is no evidence of how much that demand would be in the
absence of controls. Under the assumptions given, there would

be no reason to expect that these limitations on the demand for dollar goods could be reduced.

There probably would be a somewhat different pattern of expenditures by the importing country, since there is some joint planning of aid which would not occur on a payments-out-of-earnings basis. There is even the possibility that the substitution, because it would be deflationary in the importing country, might lead to some reduction in its foreign demand, though whether this would actually appear or not would depend upon the demand for imports which is pent up by the trade restrictions. It is worth considering whether or not both trade and aid, with the gains appearing in some relaxation of restrictions, might not be a more constructive line of policy in the immediate future.

There are certain other aspects of aid which cannot be wholly disregarded. In some few cases, aid has been given to help a government to acquire its own local currency through the sale of the aid-provided goods. If paid for in trade, no counterpart funds would have been created. Thus a government with limited budgetary resources has been enabled to finance defense development, capital expenditures, or other programs which have been regarded as desirable both by that government and by the United States administration. Although it appears as aid in the form of goods, it serves to shift funds from the private to the public sector.

There are additional instances in which the United States administration has believed that certain developments would be in the long-term interest of a particular country, but the government concerned has not thought it right or feasible itself to find the resources for this purpose. In some such instances (land reform, for example) aid has been given with the direct purpose of encouraging and enabling a government to undertake such a program. If trade were wholly substituted for aid, such possibilities would no longer exist. On the other hand, from the point of view of the recipient country, it would probably prefer to be more free in directing the use of its own resources. One cannot generalize too freely about these matters.

No matter how much a particular executive branch of a government may wish to carry out certain programs, it may be unable to find acceptable means of financing or to levy added taxes to accomplish its purpose. Aid may provide a way out, if the same programs seem important to the officials of the aiding country.

The conclusion which seems to emerge is that there are very important functions which are still performed by the dollars which are made available through nonmilitary aid, principally by way of broadening the multilateral basis of trade and facilitating economic development. If trade were substituted for aid, the burden imposed on the United States taxpayer would be lightened and the national pride of aid-receiving countries would be satisfied. More important, there would be a disappearance of the minor sources of friction which are engendered by annual negotiations of aid and by the present need for critical examination of foreign countries' economic policies before aid is approved.

But trade is clearly not a complete and equivalent substitute for aid. The possible secondary consequences discussed above would have to be borne in mind. Probably, with respect to the payments problem, trade and aid need to be evaluated separately in terms of their relation to the basic objectives sought. An expansion in trade would undoubtedly help the situation. To what extent this gain should be devoted to the liquidation of aid is another problem.

Above all, the needs of the underdeveloped countries will probably continue to be best dealt with in part at least on a basis of assistance. And it is well to keep in mind that this discussion has not related to those military shipments which we call " aid " and Europe calls our " share of the burden."

CHAPTER III

The Use and Abuse of Controls

WARS are periods during which governments of necessity greatly extend their controls over economic life both domestically and internationally. However, even before World War II, the peacetime period of the thirties saw a substantial increase in the use of government regulation and direction of economic activity as governments endeavored to cope with the unemployment situation. Since the end of the war, although many controls have disappeared like the rationing of consumer goods, most economies are still subject to widespread regulation.

In the previous chapter, controls over international transactions were discussed briefly in connection with their present use as an equilibrating device by a country in balance-of-payments difficulty (a permissible use of controls under both the International Monetary Fund and the General Agreement on Tariffs and Trade). This chapter will review some of the other justifications for and objections to controls and discriminations with respect to international transactions which are frequently put forward. More detailed analyses of particular types of controls will be found in later chapters.

THE SECURITY OBJECTIVE

The security problem today is not entirely a military problem. Security may require the deliberate non-optimum allocation of resources. With security in mind, it is surely not a matter of indifference whether war industries are located in one country (in particular, one's own country) or another. Nor are war industries the only ones of interest. It may be that the threat of shutting off the supply of imported food would appear to justify special efforts to build up domestic agriculture, be it high cost or not.

War and defense objectives can most honestly, openly, and effectively be achieved by direct subsidy. This, however, requires action through the budget, tax, and appropriations machinery; and import controls, while being taxes in effect, are concealed and therefore politically more expedient. Usually, however, import controls are merely negative and do not insure (or may even overinsure) the character and extent of economic activity which security demands. Such security as is obtained by protective devices is paid for by the consumers of the particular products concerned, rather than by the citizenry in general. There is a real danger that the government will use the cloak of security, a policy objective which cannot be challenged, to achieve other purposes. This is another reason why subsidy is usually a better approach than restriction.

Conversely, when restrictions are imposed by any country to further some national interest, they can sometimes weaken the unity of purpose which lies at the basis of any defense alliance. This is particularly true when the restrictions are imposed ostensibly for security reasons and imply an intent to build a self-sufficient military economy quite at variance with the kind of military alliance which it is trying to develop with its allies. In this positive context, symbols become important and symbolic action in fields such as trade policy can make a significant contribution to general rapprochement.

Structural Adjustments

In the effort to encourage certain types of economic activity in a country and to discourage others, various forms of controls over trade and payments may be employed. Usually justified on a temporary basis, the record shows a dangerous tendency for them to continue. Protection for an infant industry (though it probably will never admit to outgrowing the infant stage) may contribute to its rapid development, though the process is by no means automatic or assured. Multiple exchange rates offer a variety of possibilities, from giving special emphasis to building up tourism to encouraging the local processing of raw materials. The use of tariffs, quotas, and exchange controls are most effective when the effort is to replace a foreign source with a domestic source or to protect an existing domestic source.

Among the problems which arise are (1) the degree to which one can wisely " plan " an economy, (2) how much these negative actions will assure the desired positive ones, and (3) whether the encouragement or protection given will not tend to persist as a charge against the consumer long after it is needed. It is worth emphasizing that controls also are used to prevent structural adjustments. This becomes readily apparent when the question is one of removing some form of protection which has existed for some time.

The process of applying import and exchange controls may also involve the allocation of a scarce supply of foreign exchange for its " most important " uses and thus may affect not only the production pattern but the expenditure pattern. In most cases, this means giving preference to " essential " uses such as food, and excluding high-priced automobiles, washing machines, and the like. In the allocation, the servicing of foreign capital may be put far down on the list of priorities. Here there is a real deterrent to capital flow and no certainty that domestic savings will be stimulated correspondingly.

The situation is clear as to the immediate effect on the country. By denying import licenses and foreign exchange allocations for the nonessential and luxury goods demanded by the rich, the authorities can allocate more of the supply of exchange for the importation of goods for the poor. The poor will thus be able to buy more imported goods at lower prices. There is less certainty that the controls really achieve a redistribution of real income. What will be the effect on the domestic production of these items whose prices are depressed? Can the control of imports be effective in altering the distribu-

tion of real income so long as the money that is barred from
being spent for "nonessential" imports may be spent for
equally "nonessential" home products? The buying power of
the rich, turned away by the control authorities from the
foreign exchange market, can assert itself in the domestic markets. Little is accomplished for a more equitable income distribution if the luxury automobiles which would have been
acquired from abroad now take the form of less efficient but
equally expensive vehicles produced at home. And the results
may not be better if the demand for imported luxury items is
diverted to the construction of luxury villas or to more conspicuous consumption or to the purchase of foreign securities
(a common pattern in Latin America).

The most acceptable conclusion seems to be that the effectiveness of exchange controls in altering the distribution of incomes
will depend on the uses to which the funds turned away from
the foreign exchange market will be put. To the extent to
which they will be diverted to domestic capital formation (by
being spent on productive enterprises) or to disinflation (by
not being spent at all) distribution may be more equitable.
What the actual probabilities are remains indeterminate.

The object of the controls may be to change the structure
of the economy in another direction, to protect it from external
shock. Here is a new protectionism—to put it baldly, protection
from the vagaries of the American economy and the uncertainties of American policy and from the political calculations
of Russian foreign trading. It may lead to individual autarchy
or to a regional grouping endeavoring to minimize its relations
with the dollar and the ruble area. Essentially, it means developing even at higher cost home production and alternative
trade channels so far as possible. Even when there is no such
deliberate long-term plan, controls may be used as in the
thirties in the effort to shift depressions and unemployment out
of a country to other countries and, so far as possible, to protect one's borders from any such import.

Supporting Domestic Policies

Most governments recognize the necessity for maintaining high levels of employment, although just what a tolerable amount of unemployment may be, differs from country to country. This responsibility is bound to inject government action into the domestic scene, either continuously or at least from time to time, in order to maintain purchasing power. It is fairly likely that steps taken in the domestic economy will be paralleled by steps in the international field. It is, of course, possible that an increase in domestic purchasing power will lead to increased imports and a deficit in the balance of payments. The use of controls to restrict such imports and hold down prices may raise the level of employment above the point attainable without the controls, at least in the short run. This of course assumes that the reduced imports do not have a serious effect on other economies and do not in turn reduce exports and create unemployment in the export industries.

If, with the existing productive resources fully employed, effective demand for goods and services increases for any of a number of reasons at a rate much faster than the rate at which new productive resources come into existence or old resources become more productive, prices will tend to rise. It is possible in wartime, when appeals to patriotism are most effective, to retard or repress the inflation of prices. In the attempt to make wartime price controls as effective as possible, foreign trade controls are essential.

Whether it is possible and expedient in peacetime to try to suppress through direct controls a continuing inflation is highly controversial. As long as it can be reasonably expected that the inflationary pressures will soon disappear and a disinflation will become practicable, a case can be made for the temporary use of controls, including trade and exchange restrictions. But when the inflationary pressures persist and domestic price levels rise, a policy of using controls to keep imports cheap in domestic money, and yet at the same time to restrict the volume of imports, makes even more difficult and painful the readjustment that must eventually be faced (although the record of continuous inflation in some countries is notable).

Eventually domestic prices, foreign prices, and the exchange rate must come into an appropriate new relationship unless restrictive controls or subsidies are to be permanent. The ultimate adjustment after a period of inflationary pressures with full employment and a current excesss demand for foreign exchange involves a distribution of the burden between disinflation and devaluation. The less disinflation is practicable, the greater the need for devaluation or for letting the exchange rate find its level (which may mean the same thing). But no matter which adjustment policy it chooses, the government will hardly have the courage to let go of direct controls while things are so much in flux. The authorities will always be so fearful of a mass flight of capital and of speculative hoarding of foreign currencies that they will not want to do without controls. Few would argue that they ought to do otherwise.

Complications in the process of adjustment arise if there is a close tie between consumer prices and wage rates. For then the adjustment of the exchange rate, resulting in higher import prices which enter the cost-of-living index, might lead to an increase in money wage rates. Whether this is likely depends on many factors: what the ratio is between imports and national income; what part of imports consists of consumers' goods; how important these imported consumers' goods are in the cost-of-living index; what time lag there is between the price rise and the wage increase; etc. In many economies today, the danger of a wage-price spiral is serious.

One factor sometimes disregarded in this connection is the degree to which the existence of import restrictions may already have been reflected in domestic prices. It is easily possible that domestic prices of imported goods have fully expressed their scarcity value, so that the adjustment of the exchange rate merely eliminates the windfall profits of the importers or merchants but does not increase prices to consumers. In this case, one need have less fear of a new inflationary spiral. At the other extreme in influence are raw materials which are very likely to influence the entire price structure.

But if the likelihood of a rise in prices is very great, and if the price increase inevitably leads to a wage increase, and if this wage increase is not likely to be offset by an increase in productivity, and if a monetary policy to prevent an income expansion is not feasible, then it is hard to see how the reasons for maintaining trade controls can be questioned. They are merely a part of a whole structure of maladjustments. But it will still be controversial whether controls should be used in such a case to perpetuate a disequilibrium in the form of an excess demand for foreign exchange left unsatisfied by the control authorities, or to introduce an appropriate multiple-exchange-rate system, or to accomplish the devaluation but neutralize some of its domestic effects by subsidies and consumer rationing.

BARGAINING POWER

The development of an effective import and exchange control machinery in the last twenty-five years has made it possible for governments, or for economists thinking on their behalf, to consider the use of that machinery to achieve various objectives of foreign policy. Obviously, one cannot fully use the purchase of goods as bargaining counters, unless one can cut down or increase the flow according to any commitment made. There is an intermediate condition, in which the bargain may eliminate certain obstacles but not promise actual delivery, i. e., provide freedom to shop around.

Bargaining power may be used either in selling or in buying. It may be used to obtain a market to dispose of a surplus or keep a domestic industry fully employed. The price to be received for these exports may not be nearly so important as simply getting rid of an absolute volume of exports sufficient to keep certain industries going at capacity. On the other hand, bargaining power may be used to extract scarce materials from a supplier country in periods of shortage in volumes greater than the exporting country would otherwise permit.

Bargaining power may also be used for the purpose of influencing price arrangements. Getting better terms of trade means, of course, that other countries get worse terms of trade. Economic policy with such an aim has been compared to a monopolist's attempt to exploit his customers and his suppliers and has been roundly denounced as immoral and bad behavior in a good society of nations. On the other hand, it is claimed that governments should be concerned only with the interests of their own people and should let the chips fall where they may.

The Schacht policy of the Nazi government produced a network of bilateral barter agreements, each stipulating the quantities and the relative prices of products to be traded. It is said that even this attempt to take fullest advantage of control machinery, and the monopoly position which it secured, was not very successful in economic terms. Some believe that certain governments are in a position to benefit today from such international trade bargaining. However, as trade expands and more sources and markets become available, the ability of any one country to obtain preferential treatment from another country is correspondingly reduced. In any widespread use of bilateral bargaining, it is more likely that all nations would lose, owing to the discriminatory trade restrictions required of all parties concerned and the resulting retrogression in the division of labor.

It should be noted that the use of controls as a bargaining device is not necessarily limited to trade objectives. Countries may wish to apply pressure to other countries for many purposes, ranging from the desire to protect its citizens (the instances of Americans and western Europeans held behind the iron curtain) to the effort to settle nationalization claims or even to recover on defaulted private debts. It is difficult to assess the economic cost of restriction against some specific political gain. In many cases, the bargaining value of the economic threat or offer is not a particularly strong one, especially when it is offered as against some political consideration which is likely to have more emotional content. Of course, the clearest case of beneficial bargaining arises when one country

offers to reduce restrictions if and when other countries will
do the same.

STATE TRADING

The extreme form of control, state trading, carries one far
beyond the possibility of identifying objectives (not easy in
any event) and even of measuring performance. At least with
respect to tariffs, the extent of protection is fairly accurately
defined. In the case of quantitative restrictions, there is a real
possibility of identifying discrimination. To be sure, the state
trader is limited by economic facts like the elasticity of demand
but is not necessarily limited by the principle of single price,
although private traders also are sometimes in a position to use
different price policies in different markets.

Although there are a number of formulae which have been
suggested to define nondiscrimination in the case of state
trading such as current transactions proportional to the historical pattern, open bidding for purchase or sale, or pricing
and sales to be based upon " commercial considerations," none
of these has much promise of fitting state trading into the
rules of a multilateral nondiscriminating trading world. However, there is some encouragement in the fact that, for many
products, a monopoly of the participation of a single country's
trade would not have significant bargaining power. Probably
state trading is more effective in bilateral bargaining than when
faced with various alternative suppliers or buyers. It is also
encouraged by disequilibrium (the Brazil-United Kingdom
cotton-aircraft deal) .

One chain of circumstances seems to have acted as a deterrent to state trading. State trading tends to concentrate on raw
materials because these are standardized and are most manage-
able from a bulk-buyer's point of view. When the domestic
processors are not nationalized and when they find themselves
paying more than world prices for their materials, they exert
every form of political pressure to end state trading. On the
other hand, if the state is purchasing from domestic producers
at below world prices, the same forces are brought to bear by
the suppliers.

Probably the most important consideration involved in state trading is the tendency for economic considerations to be subverted to the political (foreign policy). It is a potential weapon of strong powers against small nations, state trading being a convenient and easily coordinated instrument of economic bargaining and pressure.

Some Conclusions Regarding Controls

The many different considerations involved in the use of controls make it clear that any notion that they can easily be eliminated is nonsense. They exist for a multitude of reasons, and the longer they exist, the more difficult they are to eliminate. They inevitably develop vested interests which become more and more entrenched as time passes. The possible effects on individuals and industries from the removal, absence, or change of foreign exchange controls and tariff and trade restrictions may be of many kinds. Frequently, one must weigh the benefit or cost of certain widespread but limited effects against a more intense contrary impact on certain special interests.

No close analysis is needed here of those fears of loss from the relaxation of controls which probably weigh heavily in the considerations of men of influence in a good many countries—the losses to these men themselves and to the vested interests they represent. One can hardly overestimate the will to survive and the strength to resist abolition of private and public bureaucratic organizations, especially if strong vested interests have grown up behind them. The powers that have so successfully resisted the abolition of tariff protection almost everywhere are also resisting the removal of those effective protective devices—direct import and exchange restrictions. Industrial labor and agricultural power groups are sometimes united with an entrenched bureaucracy in the fight for the maintenance of the controls. They often will not declare their particular interests in the existing institutions. But they will exploit to the fullest all the arguments that can be made on general economic or political grounds.

Furthermore, there is no doubt but that a sudden with-drawal of protection would cause difficulties, and this is an appealing argument. Suppose the productive resources in a country are fully employed and largely immobile and suppose it is therefore not possible to increase quickly the capacity to produce exportable goods, then the attainable volume of ex-ports seems to be determined by the given " structure " of the economy. If, with a removal of import and exchange con-trols, the selection of imports is suddenly left to market forces, the prices of foreign currencies will be bid up and different imports will be acquired. Domestic demand, likewise, will be differently distributed over goods and services and the given structure of the economy may not be adapted to it. Existing productive facilities may now be unsuitable and labor may become unemployed.

It should also be noted that there seems to be a basic ten-dency for controls to expand. When pressure is applied to the economy at some point, it breaks out somewhere else (like trying to squeeze a balloon). It may not break out at the desired point, so more controls are required. And, of course, there is a close relationship between domestic and foreign policy in this regard. Foreign controls, as has already been pointed out, may be required to support or to be consistent with some domestic program. Thus, United States agricultural quota restrictions are related to the character of the domestic agricultural price support program.

Nevertheless, the basic question is: Is it, or should it be, one of the central objectives of economic policy to eliminate, by making them unnecessary, the variety of limitations on trade and payments by which most of the economies of the free world are still sustained? To that question there obviously is no unani-mous answer. There is considerable agreement that the extent of controls is greater at present than most of us would wish to see remain permanently. This is related to a number of situ-ations in which there is the possibility of improvement: the present incompleteness of structural adjustment to the con-ditions of the postwar world with consequent low elasticities not only of supply but also of demand; the absence of exchange rates which press towards equilibrium in the trade and payments situation; the uncertainty as to the terms of trade; the inadequacy of gold and dollar reserves so that a country in balance-of-payments difficulties needs to be able quickly to put a brake on imports or stimulate exports; the still pent-up demands for capital in some countries, where large arrears from wartime have not been overtaken and demands for rearmament and export must be reconciled with those for re-equipment in the domestic market. In many such cases it is hoped that as structural adjustment proceeds, the need for controls will be progressively demolished.

At the same time, it is argued that in many instances controls are intended not to frustrate the working of the free economy but to achieve the same results more certainly and quickly. This is inevitably a matter on which there is considerable disagreement. It is undeniable that the right controls, efficiently and honestly operated, can in theory obtain the same results as would proceed from a free economy, and even improve on those of a free economy by limiting inflationary pressures and mitigating monopolistic tendencies.

What is not so certain is that controls will always in practice be operated wisely, efficiently, and honestly and that personal and political favoritism and even corruption will not manifest themselves. There are very natural and strongly felt objections to any system which dispenses privileges on an arbitrary basis; and even where controls seek to escape the charge of arbitrariness by using the performance of a now distant past year as a basis of allocation, the effect is the perpetuation of a past pattern and the creation of obstacles to new entry and expansion. For such reasons, there are many who hold strongly that general and impersonal fiscal and financial instruments are much to be preferred to those specific controls which attempt on the basis of individual human judgments by controllers to discriminate in the treatment of different individual producers or consumers.

From the limited information available in this field, it would appear that the efficiency and honesty with which controls are operated differ very considerably from country to country. The sense of discipline and the importance attached to equality of treatment also differ considerably. The efficacy and results of controls depend on the moral codes and behaviors of the business community: in one country restrictions of imports of consumer goods may result in abnormal profits to retailers and steep increases of prices; in another the result may be informal rationing of scarce goods by retailers who continue to sell on normal margins at an unchanged price. In one country it may be almost a matter of self-respect to circumvent the control; in another to defeat one's trade rivals by such means may be regarded as despicable. For all these reasons it is to be doubted whether there are generalizations of universal validity which can be properly applied to all countries. And it would suggest that different types of controls might be more appropriate in some countries than others, depending upon the degree of discipline and respect for law.

The above discussion leads to the conclusion that different types of trade controls might be prescribed according to the political and social discipline in the country. It should be added that the backward nature of the financial institutions and tax and other fiscal operations of some underdeveloped countries may justify at least a theoretical case for import controls. However, in such a situation it is not clear that the administrators in the trade field will be able to diminish the undesired type of imports or to keep domestic capital from escaping. Furthermore, controls are necessarily dependent upon a competent planning process and it is highly doubtful whether most civil servants are in a position to make better decisions than would individual investors. Civil servants and ministers are likely to be particularly subject to considerations of national prestige (steel mills whether economic or not) and to local pressures with regard to the location and priority of industrial development. However, there are situations in which decisions by civil servants are more likely to serve the "national interest" than the actions of private persons operating in the market place, particularly if it is an imperfect market.

To many countries, the present inadequacy of reserves, the difficulties and uncertainties of expanding and maintaining much larger exports in an increasingly competitive world, the wide oscillations of relative prices and of the terms of trade, these all appear to present a convincing argument for the retention of essential controls over imports. The obstacles to multilateral trade and clearing and the difficulties of switching purchases of imports from one source of supply to another appear to justify a discriminatory element in such control. And they can argue with some justification that the ordinary operations of a free market system—the rise of certain exchange rates, for instance, and the fall or maintenance of others—would produce almost exactly the same effects somewhat more slowly and less certainly, and would be equally discriminatory in the sense that the consequences would affect differently the country's trade with other nations.

In spite of all these considerations which seem to justify the use of controls, there are many who strongly resent and suspect such instruments of policy and believe that they represent arbitrary and unfair methods of preventing the expansion of more efficient producers at the expense of the less efficient; that such crutches as quantitative restrictions and exchange controls should be removed as quickly as possible and the weaklings forced to stand on their own legs. Under most circumstances, controls seem to be antithetical to the basic objectives of policy—greater opportunities for trade and increased multilateral trade.

Many of these questions are separately discussed in the chapters which follow. What it is here important to emphasize is that any complete solution is likely to depend on many actions in many fields. Much of the justification of controls relates to their usefulness in adjusting foreign trade in the absence of a basic production, price, and exchange rate structure which would achieve a more basic equilibrium. Therefore, a change in the use of controls is related to changes in these other factors. A partial solution of any one aspect of the problem may be almost impossible to secure, unless the countries primarily concerned see in sight a possible solution of some other problem or problems, which at present inhibit the desirable action in the first field.

Furthermore, controls by one country are related to and interlocking with the controls of other countries. Action to reduce controls can sometimes be taken by a group which could not be taken separately, as in the case of the European Payments Union. And only by group action can rules be set up which will define the appropriate uses of restrictive controls within the broader interest of the world economy.

One important difficulty is the very natural tendency to examine controls one at a time rather than to appreciate the full impact upon a country's foreign economic relations of the total set of its own controls and of their interaction with the controls of other countries. In all probability, the administrators of a control system are not themselves able to evaluate it in its full relation to the economy, let alone to the world. The degree to which exports may be affected by higher import prices (particularly if they are raw materials) ; the encouragement of capital flow into protected but uneconomic industries; and the disruption or protection of trade channels are all costs which may not be apparent on the surface. And the avoidance of controls through foreign exchange discount deals and switch trades or through resale while at sea or the exploitation of loopholes in regulation or administration all need to be taken into account in appraising any control system on an over-all basis. Probably a total evaluation would describe foreign trade and payments controls as presently necessary evils, but with disagreement about whether they always will be necessary, and whether some are as necessary as others, and whether more rapid progress cannot be made in freeing the international economy from their tendency to hamper the processes of adjustment and expansion.

CHAPTER IV

Problems of Expanding International Trade

THE CHANGES AT WORK IN INTERNATIONAL TRADE

THE major problem of the postwar period in the field of international trade has been to remove the imbalance between the United States and the rest of the world at a high enough level to permit economic progress. This problem in turn is importantly related to the level of trade among the non-dollar countries since this determines alternative sources. The imbalance with the dollar area has been most conspicuous in western Europe, which at the end of the war found itself both short of the resources for reconstruction and lagging behind the United States in the export of manufactures. No other area had been so dependent upon exporting manufactures to procure food and raw materials. The imports of the United Kingdom, for example, rose from 11 per cent of its national income in 1820 to 38 per cent in 1880; and the proportion, after falling to 22 per cent in 1937 largely because of a favorable movement in the terms of trade, rose again to 34 per cent in 1951.

During the nineteenth century, Europe did a very large proportion of world trade in manufactures. The United Kingdom, France, and Germany were still responsible for 60–65 per cent in 1913. The British share was steadily decreasing, being about 38 per cent in 1876–80 and 29 per cent in 1906–10, but it was a declining share of a more rapidly growing trade. World trade in manufactures increased threefold between 1880 and 1913.

After 1913 this substantial rate of growth came to an end. Between the wars, the volume of world trade in manufactures never appreciably exceeded that of 1913; the peak of 1926–30 was hardly above the 1913 level; the average of 1931–35 was only 76 per cent of 1913; the average of 1936–38 was 92 per cent. At the same time the shares of European countries were declining within this reduced total, while those of the United States, Canada, and Japan were increasing. The United States share was 8 per cent in 1906–10 and 16 per cent in 1926–30 and 1936–38. Japan did a negligible percentage before 1913, but reached 3.5 per cent in 1926–30 and 7 per cent in 1936–38. Even though helped by favorable terms of trade, the strains and stresses of the 1930's were in considerable part the result of the need of European countries to adjust themselves to this changing situation. Even apart from the war, they would have been forced to make considerable changes in their trade patterns.

As the result of wartime and postwar changes in assets and earning position, almost all the chief trading countries of Europe were confronted with the necessity of increasing their exports of manufactures by 50 to 100 per cent if they were to balance their payments. But since collectively they did 50 per cent of the world trade before the war and another 27 per cent was in the hands of the United States, Canada, and Japan, the prospects were not bright for them to meet their need for imports by increasing their shares in world trade in manufactures. Very much, therefore, depended on what might happen to the total volume of that trade.

A number of circumstances have brought about a dramatic reversal of the interwar trend and the volume of world trade in manufactures has risen at an unprecedented rate approximately as follows:

1937	100	1951	172
1948	120	1952	170
1949	128	1953	173
		(First Quarter)	

As a result, countries have been able to secure increases of almost 75 per cent without the necessity of increasing their shares in the total trade.

The shares of different countries have not, however, remained constant. The changes that have occurred have been estimated as follows.[1]

DISTRIBUTION OF EXPORT TRADE
IN MANUFACTURED GOODS

	1937	1951	1952
	Per Cent of Total		
United States	16.6	26.1	28.0
Canada	4.2	4.5	5.1
Japan	6.1	0.9	0.8
United Kingdom	19.1	20.2	19.0
Western Germany	13.3	8.0	8.3
France	5.4	8.2	7.3
Belgium	5.0	3.3	3.0
Sweden	2.1	1.9	1.8
Switzerland	2.4	2.2	2.3
Italy	3.1	2.2	1.9
Others [a]	22.5	22.5	22.5
Total	*100.0*	*100.0*	*100.0*

[a] Actual for 1937; assumed constant in later years.

The increases in the United States and Canadian shares have been at the expense of western Europe and Japan. The group of seven European countries, which did 50.4 per cent of the trade in 1937, did only 46.0 per cent in 1951 and 43.6 per cent in 1952. Thus their collective success in earning additional foreign exchange through the export of manufactured goods depends heavily on the expansion of world trade.

[1] Austin Robinson, "The Future of British Imports," *The Three Banks Review* (March, 1953), 8.

There is a serious danger that world trade in manufactures may now begin to contract and that countries which make their living through such exports may be faced with increased difficulties. The great increase in trade in manufactures since the war has been due to the need to replace capital and other durable goods worn out during the war years, the favorable terms of trade enjoyed by primary producers which have supported their demand for manufactured goods, the high level of industrial expansion and capital investment throughout the world, and, not least, the existence of United States aid in all its various forms. Of these factors, the first, and to some extent the fourth, are coming to an end and the second is now much less powerful; in addition, Japan and Western Germany are certain to add to the supply of manufactured goods and to bring their shares of the total much nearer to prewar proportions, with consequent reductions in the share of other countries.

Furthermore, it should be noted that the proportion of total manufacturing production entering international trade declined during the recovery of the late thirties and during the postwar period. This implies an increased dependence of the industrial countries on imported raw materials as well as a greater measure of self-sufficiency in other countries in manufactured goods because of the growth of local industries. The records of changing products and shifting trade patterns should be examined if one hopes to evaluate the trends at all exactly. Many specific developments can be listed, but much more study is needed before one can judge their permanence or persistence. The extraordinary changes in wheat and rice sources, the United States expansion in textiles, the battle of automobile design, the increase in the export of parts rather than finished goods, the attempts to encourage at least first stage processing in raw material producing countries, and the impact of economic development—all are factors of substantial importance. Nor is there adequate evidence as to the international prejudices of technical experts, the loyalty of buyers to former trade names and trading partners, or the importance of technological prestige. These all will play some part in fixing the national shares in the market of the future.

The difficulties experienced by western Europe in achieving a satisfactory pattern of trade are bound up also with the willingness of other areas of the world to trade with it and the terms on which such trade can be carried on. The increased dependence of western Europe on America in the postwar period is largely a reflection of its difficulties in obtaining supplies from other parts of the world. This is true, for example, of its trade with eastern Europe which, even before it was somewhat restricted for reasons of security, had greatly contracted because the goods normally obtained from that area were either not available or available only on a limited scale. The program to build up industry in the East and to link the satellites more firmly with the Soviet bloc in a self-sufficient whole has obliged western Europe to rely even more on dollar sources for supplies of wheat, coarse grains, fats and oils, soft woods, and coal. It is probable also that the move toward autarchy in the East has forced western Europe to trade on less favorable terms.

The reduction in the trade between western and eastern Europe has been substantial. Valued at 1948 prices, recorded imports into western Europe fell from $3.1 billions in 1938 to $1.16 billions in 1948 and $0.85 billion in 1951. Exports from western Europe fell from $1.6 billions in 1938 to $0.8 billion in 1948 and $0.7 billion in 1951. However, there probably is substantial clandestine trade in strategic goods. Trade between China and western Europe had never been of much significance but has fallen by 50 per cent since the imposition of an embargo on strategic goods by the United Nations.

It would greatly exaggerate the importance of these reductions in trade with eastern Europe to regard them as measuring the burden placed on the western European countries. Western Europe would have paid for increased volumes of eastern European imports in part with dollar earning or dollar saving goods, e. g., machinery and transportation equipment. In addition, western Europe had always supplied eastern

Europe with considerable amounts of goods like automobiles, machine tools, and spare parts which were bought in turn from the United States. At a time when western Europe's productive facilities were almost fully employed, these circumstances might have meant that increased imports from eastern Europe would not have greatly helped western Europe's balance-of-payments situation.

For the free world as a whole the physical replacement of goods previously purchased in eastern Europe (with the exception perhaps of softwoods) is not a very difficult adjustment to make; but it can be made only if corresponding changes are made in the markets to which western Europe has access. It implies a greater volume of exports of manufactures to non-European destinations where the obstacles to the entry of European goods are likely to be greater and the competitive advantages of European manufactures are certainly less than they used to be in eastern Europe. The case of Yugoslavia is, of course, the extreme illustration of the difficulties of reorienting one's trade channels.

It is not, however, the scale of the reduction in East-West trade that is significant. In relation to total imports into western Europe of over $30 billions, eastern Europe is not nearly as important as other areas of supply. For some European countries such as Denmark, Austria, and Western Germany, the decline in East-West trade has consequences of a quite different order of magnitude. For nearly all, it has a significance not to be measured in proportions—it throws them into an increased dependence on other continents for the necessities of life and obliges them to find new markets either in North America or in competition with American manufactures. The decline of East-West trade has been one of the factors causing the terms of trade to turn against western Europe and to increase the deficit of western Europe with North America.

For a number of commodities such a realignment of the pattern of trade has been discernible. Of the wheat imports of the five chief European importers,[2] 39 per cent came from the dollar area in 1934–38 while 13 per cent came from eastern Europe. In 1951, 76 per cent came from the dollar area and less than 2 per cent from eastern Europe. An important further strain on the dollar resources of Europe springs from the diminished supplies now available from Latin American sources, especially Argentina; Latin America provided 21 per cent of the wheat total in 1934–38 and only 6 per cent in 1951. Very similar realignments have occurred with other commodities.

The Economic Commission for Europe has tried to quantify the new problems faced by western Europe since 1938. Using the 1938 volume of commodity exports as a basis, it estimated that income on external assets dropped from 32 per cent prewar to 9 per cent in 1950–51, and that new indebtedness would require additional foreign payments equivalent to about 6 to 7 per cent. Terms of trade were estimated to have worsened by 25 per cent, representing an added burden of 44 per cent on exports (since the commodity export base was much smaller than the import base). Adding an allowance for declines in some other sources of invisible income, it estimated that, if the adjustment were to be entirely in the form of commodity exports, their volume would need to be some 80 per cent greater than in 1938 in order to pay for the same volume of imports as in that year. This is the same as saying that the adjustment for these changes would require export increases or import reductions from the 1938 levels of trade of western European countries totalling about $8 billions per annum (valued at 1952 prices).

The burden of adjustment has been greatly eased by the aid furnished by the United States. That the burden has been no light one is evident from the structural change that has been forced on a country like the United Kingdom which exported about 70 per cent more in volume in 1952 than in 1938,

[2] United Kingdom, Germany, Italy, Belgium, and the Netherlands. See *Economic Survey of Europe since the War*, United Nations, Geneva (1953), Table **XXXVII**, 284.

imported about 15 per cent less, and yet had only a small favorable over-all balance of payments.

THE PRODUCTIVITY FACTOR

But if the trade and payments problem is in part the result of the imperfect adjustment of the various economies to their postwar conditions, may there not be a continually disturbing factor in the differing rates of increase of productivity in different countries? (Productivity is used here in the over-all factor sense, assuming that labor saving is not offset by added capital cost.) There is little satisfactory evidence on changing productivity differentials—is the rate of growth of productivity currently more rapid in the United States than in Europe?—nor is it clear whether or not the changes are concentrated in industries where they tend to aggravate or ease balance-of-payments problems. For example, an increase in productivity in a non-export industry will obviously not increase exports but may tend to increase real income and hence imports.

If we assume that the productivity improvement leads to lower prices, that foreign demands are elastic, but that progress is also made in the import-competing sectors, it then is necessary to evaluate the substitution effect against the income effect. However, other factors must be considered. A relative increase in productivity in one country would probably lead at least in part to an increase (though not necessarily proportional) in its money wage rates. If one assumes a slower adjustment in wages than in prices, countries with relatively rapid rates of increased productivity will tend to have surpluses in their balance of payments (unless they happen to export products with an inelastic demand). This analysis undoubtedly magnifies the importance of productivity changes. It is important to note that both the level of productivity and the rate of money wages affect a country's price level (and hence its trade balance), and in recent times the greatest fluctuations have come from money wage-level changes as the result of inflationary forces and of trade union power, high profits, and high marginal income tax rates.

It is not always clear as to what is cause and what is effect. For example, suppose a country is making a major effort to develop and obtains substantial technical assistance. The technological basis for a rapid advance in productivity might then be present, but nothing happens in the statistical record until it is able to apply this knowledge. Its effort to achieve its goal and to exploit the technological possibilities with which it has become familiar might put a substantial strain on its payments position. And the more it succeeded in adding to its capital resources from abroad, the more it would record an advance in productivity.

The effect of a productivity differential may be variously distributed between two trading countries, depending largely upon whether or not it narrows or widens the situation relative to comparative advantage. It is quite possible that a country may suffer actual loss of real income if the other country improves in the efficiency of its industries which formerly had a comparative disadvantage. However, the analyses based on a two-country model may be somewhat misleading in analyzing both the balance-of-payments and the real income effect of productivity changes, since the realistic case often involves adjustments in country A to productivity increases in country B when both are competing in the markets of country C.

If one assumes that part of the problem is the relatively rapid rise in United States productivity and that the industries affected and the demands involved are such as to encourage exports and diminish imports (a set of assumptions which cannot be evaluated), there seem to be at least six possible ways in which the adjustment can be made.

First is by speeding up productivity advance in other countries, which will be discussed in a later chapter. Second is for the United States to disinvest in those of its industries which have lagged in productivity and for other countries to increase their investment in those same industries (as outlined in comparative advantage analysis). Third is by increasing money wages in the United States, a tendency which is present but with relation to which productivity is only one element. Fourth is reducing wages elsewhere, a procedure involving deflation and exceedingly difficult to do politically. Fifth is by exchange rate adjustment, which in this case would presumably require gradual depreciation of other currencies against the dollar without corresponding wage-price adjustment. Sixth is to balance trade and payments by other devices—controls or aid. As to the over-all problem, it seems not to have been particularly troublesome in the past, although it certainly existed and it may prove to be unimportant in the future in the face of the increased efforts to distribute and apply technical assistance and the wide gap available in which the less advanced countries can make progress rather easily.

It may also be suggested that exports and imports may be differently affected as the result of one country's persistently developing new products. There can be no question about the importance of the extraordinary increase in the use of nylon on the silk-producing countries, of synthetic fibres on cotton and wool producers, of cellophane on wood pulp products, of frozen foods and new types of containers on the demand for tin, and of synthetic rubber upon natural rubber. Plastics have expanded tremendously. In every one of these new products, the United States has been the chief developer and in every case it has increased American exports and reduced American imports. Innovation is costly, but the American market is large enough to carry the experimental and developmental costs from which foreign purchasers may benefit. More generally, rapid progress is often associated with technical leadership; this in turn creates a demonstration effect so that the products of the country enjoying leadership are more desired even if they are at some price disadvantage.

Terms of Trade

It is important to recognize the tremendous importance of terms of trade on the trade and payments situation. Not only have raw material price swings been the greatest factor in the situation of individual countries like Australia, Brazil, and

Bolivia, but they are most important in defining the economic relationship between primary producing (mostly underdeveloped) and industrial countries. (In this instance, the United States and the OEEC countries tend to be in the same situation except for the price-of-gold component.) The terms of trade have been strongly against the industrial countries in the postwar period when compared with earlier periods. For the United States, for example, export prices rose to double the prewar level by 1948 and were at 202 in July, 1953 (1936–38 = 100), while import prices were more than three times prewar for eight months of 1951 and were at 276 in July, 1953.

The importance of swings from year to year is indicated by the recent record of the United Kingdom as follows (1952 = 100) :

	Import prices	*Export prices*	*Terms of trade*
June, 1950	76	81	95
June, 1951	102	95	108
June, 1952	100	100	100
August, 1953	87	96	91

What may be expected as to the future terms of trade is by no means clear. The extreme was reached in 1951 as the result of the raw material price rises after the attack on South Korea, since when the situation has improved considerably (from the point of view of the industrial countries). It is not difficult to agree with Colin Clark that manufactured goods can be expanded and their costs can be lowered more easily than raw materials and that over time the primary product producers cannot help but gain in the commodity terms of trade. The recent period has been one in which full employment policy plus the need to earn foreign exchange have caused a higher rate of expansion in manufacturing while the production of primary products has expanded only by some 20 per cent since 1938. It is possible that the gap may be narrowed through an increase in the output of foodstuffs and raw materials, but it also can be argued that the most likely future expansion will continue to be in the manufactures field, not to mention the effect of the increased use of synthetics.

Another approach would suggest that primary producers, in their great desire to increase their foreign earning power in order to be able to obtain more capital goods for their development, will increase production even though the demand for their products is relatively inelastic and thus their terms of trade will deteriorate. Another factor may be a more rapid population increase in the underdeveloped areas, which may lead to greater relative demand for finished goods since they probably have a more elastic demand relative to income than do primary products.

At any rate, some of the primary producing countries which have gained from these price changes have shown a strong tendency to do much of their planning in the direction of reducing imports rather than in planning increases in exports; and many of those which have stepped up their imports have turned to North America for supplies. Thus the western European countries, on the one hand, have found themselves forced to purchase in the United States when they might have hoped for additional supplies from elsewhere and, on the other, have had greater difficulty in developing a market for their manufactures than might have seemed likely. So far as the situation results from shortages of European exports associated with inflation and from delays in building up export capacity in the main industries with good export prospects, it is possible that an improvement will come about automatically as inflationary pressures are overcome and shorter delivery dates for European goods are quoted. But if the new price relationship represents a structural change connected, for example, with the efforts of primary producers to industrialize or with a growing preference for United States goods, the achievement of a multilateral pattern in which western Europe can remain in balance without aid is likely to involve intense competition in third markets between European and American manufacturers, a further movement in the terms of trade against Europe, and a corresponding burden on European industry.

The division of trade between certain European and American exports in the markets of third countries and in one another's market is shown below. (Manufactured goods represent close to 70 per cent of the total exports of both United States and western Europe to third markets.)

EXPORT MANUFACTURED GOODS FROM OEEC COUNTRIES AND UNITED
STATES TO THIRD COUNTRIES AND TO ONE ANOTHER
JANUARY–SEPTEMBER 1952

	Exports from OEEC Countries to Third Countries	Exports from United States to Third Countries	Exports from OEEC Countries to United States	Exports from United States to OEEC Countries
	Millions of Dollars			
Chemicals	743	518	102	121
Machinery & Transport	2824	3297	137	478
Nonelectric machinery	1195	2088	80	326
Electric machinery & apparatus	615	420	10	63
Transport equipment	1013	789	47	90
Other Manufactured Goods	3250	1304	488	304
Textiles	1134	364	114	19
Base metals	891	389	228	220
Miscellaneous Manufactures	588	1042	159	57
Total	*7405*	*6161*	*886*	*960*

Source: OEEC Statistical Bulletin.

If the western European countries are to endeavor to wipe out their external deficits through increased exports rather than through cuts in imports, they will almost certainly have to fight for a bigger share of the world market in manufactures. Prices are important in this picture. If European countries wish to increase their exports of manufactures so as to bring in an additional $1 billion in export proceeds and as the price of success have to offer their exports on terms 20 per cent cheaper, they would find themselves required to ship a volume of exports to these markets more than 40 per cent larger than before. Conceivably, the lower prices might result in some offsetting expansion in demand. But what is the reaction of their competitors in the meantime? If the trade is taken away from American exporters, it would involve an even greater cut in American volume, perhaps 45 per cent. No such change is at all likely. But this illustration shows that what might seem a very modest target, equivalent to a 10 per cent increase in annual exports in value terms from western Europe to third markets, involves a tremendous disturbance in existing channels of trade unless it is achieved under conditions of rapid trade expansion. It is made even more difficult if one recalls that perhaps half the items included in the aggregates are noncompetitive for one reason or another.

Herein lay the real significance of the devaluations of 1949. The effects of these, whatever the occasion that prompted them, was to put the European countries that devalued in a better position in third markets in competition with the industrial countries which did not devalue like the United States. The effects of the devaluations were obscured by the outbreak of war in Korea shortly afterwards, but the movement of wages and prices has not been at so different a pace in the United States and the principal European industrial countries as to destroy more than a limited proportion of the competitive advantage that devaluation brought.

THE POSTWAR PLAN

Planning for the postwar world became active in 1942. The prewar trading world had been dominated by the depression, during which time various countries had attempted to support home employment by keeping out foreign goods, by increased trade restrictions, and by encouraging export by devaluations. It was an era of trying either to get ahead of the other fellow or to retaliate because of his efforts to do the same thing. There was very little international consultation, the London Economic Conference of 1933 having foundered on the problem of exchange rate stabilization and the Economic Committee of the League of Nations having no official United States member.

The planning for the postwar world was based upon the

idea that the nations would agree on certain policies in advance and would establish permanent international organizations to act as the center for future international cooperation in each particular field. The planners knew the world which lay behind them but did not fully anticipate the nature and extent of the problems which would appear in the postwar world. It was originally envisaged at Bretton Woods and at the conferences which developed the Charter for the International Trade Organization that trade in the postwar world would, after a period of transition, be regulated by general agreements operating within a framework of convertibility of currencies and multilateral trade.

Because convertibility was assumed, nondiscrimination was taken as the normal state of affairs from which departures were to be permitted only in exceptional circumstances. Because nondiscrimination was taken as the starting point, tariffs were accepted as a permissible form of government intervention in international trade (so long as they were not discriminatory among countries except where preferences already existed), while on the other hand quantitative limitations by quota or license were treated as undesirable aberrations calling for special justification. This idea was supported by the feeling that the market mechanism would have a freer play if it had to overcome tariff barriers than if it had to overcome quantitative restrictions, and by an antipathy to controls which permitted administrative discretion and variability.

The world turned out to be decidedly different or at least the period of transition proved to be an extremely long one, as yet far from ended. The postwar restrictions on international trade in most countries proved to be quantitative and discriminatory, largely because currencies were not in fact convertible, and thus turned on the imbalance in international economic relationships. The eyes of many were cast with disapproval on the United States tariff, against which no objection can be found in the agreements. The institutions devised at Bretton Woods made no provision for a world of inconvertible currencies; there was no machinery within the general agreements of the International Monetary Fund or the International Trade Organization for limiting the damage done by discrimination and for permitting a group of countries to use it jointly to remove a common deficit. (Possibly the " scarce currency " clause might so qualify, but it remains unused in fact.)

Currencies were assumed to be at either extreme of the range between hard and soft; if any one currency was inconvertible it was assumed to be so in isolation from the others so that the re-establishment of convertibility was a task for that country alone. But in fact the situation is usually more complicated. One country may struggle towards convertibility by pushing another back, each of a group of countries being related oligopolistically to the others—is it really sensible in such circumstances to posit the kind of atomistic response to a common deficit with North America that the rules of the International Monetary Fund presuppose? A country with an inconvertible currency may find itself in surplus with a country with a still softer currency—is the first country to be obliged, as the rules of the Fund seem to oblige it, to maintain the value of the softer currency by maintaining an unbroken cross-rate and to go on accumulating the surplus?

The postwar planning therefore provided little planning for the transition period. In fact, for situations of " balance-of-payments difficulties," it granted exceptions to the various rules of respectable international economic behavior but gave no guidance as to how to get out of them. To be sure, the reconstruction period was to be eased by the operations of UNRRA and later by loans from the International Bank for Reconstruction and Development. But essentially, it was assumed that each country would rapidly put its economic house in order. There was no real international program to facilitate the process.

MULTILATERAL TARIFF REDUCTIONS

Substantial progress has been made in one field on a broad multilateral basis, namely, in reducing tariffs. The General Agreement on Tariffs and Trade (GATT) brought into being the trade chapter of the International Trade Organization Charter on a provisional basis, which like the " transition period " still persists. In various trade agreement negotiations held under the auspices of GATT, tariff barriers have been lowered on the basis of reciprocity.

Reciprocity is of course another concept which relates to a world in balance rather than to one faced with imbalance. Its justification has always been the two-way expansion of trade. But in a case where trade in at least one direction is limited by quantitative restrictions, the effect of lowering tariffs on both sides is not so immediately clear. If tariffs are lowered in a negotiation between the United States and France, the lowered tariffs in the United States will presumably mean an increase in United States imports from France; France will have more dollars to spend; her quantitative restrictions can be correspondingly eased; and more American goods will flow to France. In such a situation, even a unilateral drop in the United States tariff would result in a two-way expansion of trade. But what is the result of the French tariff cut on purchases of American goods? Since the volume of imports into France is fixed by quantitative restrictions determined according to French capacity to pay (dollar earnings) , the tariff which was paid in francs is now redistributed somewhere among the producer, exporter, importer, and the consumer, and the suppressed demand for the product may even be increased if the franc price is lower. Therefore the concessions obtained by the creditor country may not be of immediate benefit to it.

Although not immediately important, the reciprocal action may be helpful because tariffs tend to be more difficult to deal with than many of the other forms of trade restriction. Although quantitative restrictions are undoubtedly used for many purposes other than to meet balance-of-payments difficulties, these other uses are circumscribed in the General Agreement and the Articles of Agreement of the IMF. At least it can be hoped that if and as conditions improve, these other forms of restrictions will become less prevalent, and then the level of tariff rates in the non-dollar area will be a matter of real significance. In fact, this has already happened among the EPU members in connection with their trade liberalization program.

Between 1948 and 1951, great strides were taken under GATT in reducing the level of import duties. Since 1951, there have been only a few isolated instances of decreases and the latest report of GATT shows something of a trend toward the imposition of higher protective and fiscal duties. The various reciprocal reductions in tariffs have created a situation in which some countries have only very limited tariffs remaining while others still have substantial tariff barriers. Obviously, it is impossible for them to bargain much further on the old basis of specific reciprocity.

A number of proposals for further multilateral tariff reduction have been put forward for discussion in OEEC or at GATT. One important proposal known as the French Plan is for a reduction in tariff rates by 30 per cent over a period of three years at the rate of 10 per cent in each year. A common tariff classification into 10 to 15 categories would be adopted and a maximum ad valorem rate of duty would be fixed for each category.[3] There would also be a lower limit for each category below which no reduction in duty would be called for. Each year, the average tariff rates within each sector would be reduced by 10 per cent. The choice of items for reduction within any sector would be at the discretion of each participating country. This proposal, if accepted, would give rise to no bilateral negotiations of tariff concessions but would be adopted by all countries simultaneously. It would be necessary to agree both on tariff categories, no easy matter, and on the maximum and minimum rates to be established.

A variant of this plan involves the progressive reduction of tariffs on a common list of products with a view to making

[3] This proposal was modified in September, 1953, to set the maximum rates according to four new categories, i. e., agricultural products, raw materials, semi-manufactures, and manufactures. Also, a formula was adopted in accordance with which the required average reduction varies from zero to 30 per cent depending upon the present height of the country's tariff.

these products free both of tariffs and of quantitative restrictions. This proposal, which in some ways echoes the line of thinking behind the Schuman Plan, is aimed at creating a single market, generally thought of by its protagonists as a European market, so as to allow for greater international specialization in the products on the common list.

One specific question in this field of multilateral action is particularly troublesome, that of Japan. Japan is faced with a most difficult problem of economic survival with the necessity to import food and raw materials in the face of restricted markets for Japanese products. At least temporarily, her trading activities with China are limited under the East-West trade embargo. She is aided by tremendous off-shore expenditures of the United States, related to the Far Eastern military situation. Two years ago, Japan asked for membership in the General Agreement on Tariffs and Trade. This would mean that after trade agreement negotiations with the present members, Japanese goods would receive most-favored-nation treatment in markets where they are now being discriminated against, as well as the prospect that some markets would be opened through the negotiations themselves.

Within the GATT, the proposal was viewed with less than enthusiasm by many of the industrial countries who saw additional troubles for themselves in any increase in competition in third markets, with real enthusiasm by some countries interested primarily in being able to buy abroad as cheaply as possible, and with decidedly mixed feelings by the United States representatives, torn between the fear of competition by Japanese goods in the United States market itself and the belief that the political independence of Japan can only survive if it has a reasonably solid economic base. Among the interesting technical problems is that of what concessions should Japan be required to make if she is fully admitted to GATT, in the light of the fact that she will receive the benefits of all the previous negotiations among the members.[4]

[4] At the September, 1953, meeting of GATT, Japan was invited to participate in GATT without vote and individual countries were given

THE MULTILATERAL ESTABLISHMENT OF RULES

The postwar planning also was directed towards the establishment of international rules with respect to national behavior in the commercial policy field. After prolonged negotiation, agreement was reached by national representatives on the International Trade Charter with respect to various principles and practices looking toward nondiscrimination and expanding trade. In special circumstances such as balance-of-payments difficulties or the desire of underdeveloped countries to use protection for infant industries, exceptions were provided under a degree of control by the central organization. However, the failure of the United States to ratify the Charter has meant that its only effectiveness, except for its educational value, has come through the GATT, which has operated through United States administrative acceptance under the authority of the Reciprocal Trade Agreements Act. Thus GATT has no basis in American legislation corresponding to that of the other international agencies like the International Monetary Fund.

There is obviously room for a wide difference of view as to the rigor with which common rules of commercial policy should be devised and enforced. Some would take a strong line, particularly against discriminatory practices. They would deplore any preoccupation with monetary devices and " payments gadgets " as calculated to lead to avoidance of the really awkward adjustments in any economy and away from the strict path of nondiscriminatory rectitude. There is certainly force in the view that once everybody starts to seek for an easement to domestic difficulties by utilizing trade restrictions, and particularly by restrictions that are openly discriminatory, it can become almost hopeless to try to work out a common code of commercial conduct, and the hope disappears of expanding trade or of achieving the best pattern of resource use. The idea of a code was to prevent this spiral from ever starting.

---

the option to extend most-favored-nation commitments to Japan in exchange for like commitments from Japan.

The GATT, in spite of its provisional status, has already demonstrated the usefulness of an international agency in the trade field. A number of problems of interpretation and application of the terms of the General Agreement have been settled more or less happily. It has dealt with such specific technical problems as whether or not various types of sardines were " like commodities," whether or not various seemingly internal taxes were in fact discriminatory against imported goods, and whether or not certain tariff rate coefficients were justified by changes in the exchange rate. Where the limit may prove to be in various countries, when domestic objectives clash with international commitments, is not clear. The United States has carefully explained its various escape clause actions to the GATT, and in the case of these restrictions, admitted that its action was such as to permit retaliatory action by other countries. When Congress called for the termination of the United States trade agreement with Czechoslovakia, the United States asked permission of the other members of GATT before taking the action. And the United Kingdom, desiring to raise certain tariffs indirectly bound under the GATT, accepted a limitation on its action established in the form of the GATT approval.

The policies advanced by the GATT are by no means fully accepted by all countries (Chapter II has already pointed out many of the arguments for and against the use of controls) . It has been suggested that, rather than to try to develop a detailed set of rules, it would be more helpful to establish an organization which would be concerned with a set of problems rather than the application of a particular set of articles or phrases. The argument in favor of detailed commitments is that they would be obtained before countries become actively engaged in some specific situation involving the policy issue. But the contrary position is that the agreed articles may not be fully appropriate to the actual circumstances in which the question arises and may even stand in the way of meeting the problem for which the rules were established. There is some reason to feel that one of the reasons for the effectiveness of such loosely developed organizations as the OEEC and the International Materials Conference was that the principals were able to devote their energies to substance rather than to form.

It should further be noted that, although the problems of trade and payments which have emerged in the postwar world are closely woven together, they are dealt with by two separate organizations, GATT and IMF. Although they appear to have cooperated well together, the division between tariff and trade policy on the one hand and monetary policy on the other is extremely arbitrary, and in the plans originally submitted at Bretton Woods no dividing line was drawn. Trade restrictions and exchange controls are often interchangeable. In the OEEC it has been found indispensable to marry the two in order to make the EPU a workable instrument. If it is concluded that both organizations have built up such entrenched positions with the passage of time, and that the differences between them are too great (voting power, nature of organization, and different back-stopping in each country), at least it might be possible to establish some sort of high-level committee to co-ordinate the policies and activities of the two organizations.

Possible Courses of Action

It is obvious that multilateralism, nondiscrimination, and convertibility remain a goal rather than an achievement of the postwar world. The transition period is not yet over and restrictions are still the basis for meeting balance-of-payments difficulties. The problem therefore is how to make it possible to reduce aid and eliminate these restrictions.

In the growth of multilateral trade in the nineteenth century and especially the development of the new countries in the Western Hemisphere and in the British Commonwealth, the United Kingdom occupied a central position that was almost as dominating as that now occupied by the United States. It has often been emphasized that the essential feature of the nineteenth century system was the steady expansion in the British market for the exports of the countries undergoing development, and in particular the almost uninterrupted rise in the volume of food imports into Britain. The British market set the pace for the development of primary production throughout the world and the growth of trade hinged on the readiness of that market to absorb a mounting volume of imports.

In the twentieth century the world is less confident of the need or willingness of the United States to absorb a rising volume of imports and in its own capacity to cope with any temporary setback originating there. It is not that United States imports have failed to increase quite remarkably since prewar years. Dollar payments for goods and services (excluding altogether dollars supplied by United States aid or foreign investment) averaged $14.0 billions in the years 1950–52 compared with only $3.1 billions in 1936–38, and even in real terms the increase has been nearly 50 per cent. The doubts that are felt relate to the continuation of this trend and the abruptness with which it can be reversed either by further restrictions on imports or by even a comparatively slight drop in the level of American production. It is difficult for the rest of the world to gear its plans of economic development to the expectation of a rising level of world trade if it has no assurance of a rising level of United States imports.

If, for example, the United States were to admit manufactured goods more freely, this would by itself lessen the kind of change in the terms of trade that might arise if sales of manufactures were to be pressed on third markets. Since the possible imports of manufactures is small in relation to the size of the total market for manufactures in the United States, the impact of additional imports would be felt on a broad front and not be concentrated in some smaller market where the real competition is largely between goods imported from one country and goods imported from another.

Or again, if the United States were to buy more from or lend more to primary producing countries, the immediate effect on other industrial countries would be less advantageous but their chance of finding a market for their manufactures would probably improve, particularly if the primary producers had sufficient confidence in trade to retard their schemes for

local industries. It might be possible for the primary producing and industrial countries to work out a basis for mutual
trade that would allow industrialization to proceed in the
former without preventing the steady growth of an export
surplus in primary products.

Yet no action on the part of the United States to establish
the framework of an expanding world economy can be successful if the rest of the world pursues mistaken policies. The
structural adjustments called for in the trade of western Europe
will be delayed or frustrated if inflation is allowed to divert
resources from the task of building up exports. The adjustments will never be sufficient to permit an unrestricted balance
with North America if the barriers erected against dollar imports serve, not to give time for export potential to be created,
but to create a high cost area that cannot even stand up to
competition in its own market, much less venture out and meet
competition in markets overseas. It is one thing to create the
incentives necessary to adapt the pattern of European resources
to the new position of Europe in the world and allow these
incentives time to take effect, quite another to offer indefinite
protection.

Nor is it only in western Europe that countries may pursue
mistaken policies. The commercial policies of underdeveloped
countries are often successful in restricting international trade
without providing any real advantage to their own economic
development. The theoretical justifications for such restrictions as an aid to economic development vary in novelty and
validity; but as a matter of hard fact the restrictions often fail
to promote development where circumstances do not already
favor it. If limited imports enter, it may be at a windfall
profit to the middleman and with some diversion of effort into
the operation of a black market; if the imports do not enter,
local production at high cost may be stimulated when the whole
object was to cut down expenditure on imported luxuries in
order to assist development in some quite different industry.

Basically, the situation requires policies in many countries
which will be consistent with each other and which will look

in the same direction. In the meanwhile, progress has been made in expanding trade, much of which has been through more limited approaches, some of which will be discussed in the next chapter. Also, it is important to remember that only for the purpose of analysis should trade policy be considered separately from monetary policy. They can supplement or they can defeat each other.

CHAPTER V

Areas of Trade Liberalization

IF one reviews the world scene from the point of view of trade liberalization, it is clear that postwar progress has been limited. Although the hoped for international agency, the International Trade Organization, has not materialized, the General Agreement on Tariffs and Trade has operated as a stopgap and has succeeded in lowering tariffs substantially through a revolutionary device, that of multilateral trade agreement negotiation. It has had considerable effect in maintaining certain rules and policies in the field of commercial policy which were incorporated in the General Agreement. But there are certain areas within the totality which deserve special discussion.

WESTERN EUROPE

Although a number of closer groupings have been attempted in western Europe since the war, the main regional grouping in this area, the Organization for European Economic Cooperation (OEEC), embraces all western European countries except Finland, Spain, and Yugoslavia. This organization, launched in order to give effect to the European Recovery Program, has continued even though the ERP as such has come to an end. Through the European Payments Union (which has the same membership) and the various committees of the Organization, it seeks to secure a harmonization of the economic and financial policies of its members. In this chapter, the trade aspects of its activity will be emphasized, the financial being discussed in Chapter VII.

80

In 1947, trade among the European countries was only 55 per cent of prewar level because of the existence of severe shortages in most commodities, the substantial accumulated demand within each country, and an unwillingness to hazard their limited foreign exchange reserves. As a result, each country tried to husband its own resources and to trade by exchanging less essential goods for those of greater importance to it. Trade was tightly controlled and was carried on under carefully negotiated one-year bilateral agreements. There were substantial interests which preferred such a system in order to maintain assured markets, bargain for raw materials, and limit competition from foreign sources of supply.

The OEEC found itself faced at an early stage with the need to break through this deadlock and put European trade on a more multilateral basis. This problem was recognized in the European Recovery Program by the dividing of Economic Cooperation Administration grants into direct grants and conditional grants, the latter being related to financing bilateral deficits in intra-European trade. From this, there developed a system with some transferability of such financing and in 1950 the European Payments Union was established. This provided a system of clearing and credit extension. At the same time, the OEEC sponsored the mutual and simultaneous relaxation of trade restrictions, the degree of relaxation expected from each member being raised progressively.

The movement towards the removal of quantitative restrictions on intra-European trade is generally referred to as " liberalization." No country was required to remove the restrictions limiting imports of similar goods from outside the area, nor was any country obliged to lower or even to stabilize its tariffs. It was quite consistent with the letter though not the spirit of liberalization that a country should remove quantitative restrictions on some items and simultaneously raise its tariff on these items. However, since the same countries were members of GATT, they were bound by tariff commitments made in the various trade agreements and therefore had limited freedom to take action in the tariff field. Such liberalization among the members, by lowering barriers to each other's trade, increased discrimination against non-member countries though it did not increase the barriers against them.

Each currency ranked equally within the EPU. The only deficit that mattered was the cumulated deficit of a country with the EPU—not its bilateral deficits with individual members. Hence the setting up of the EPU removed the incentive for any one member to discriminate on balance-of-payments or currency grounds against any other member. It might desire to discriminate and to enter into bilateral agreements for some other purpose, for example, to gain an assured market for one of its products or to obtain preferential access to raw materials, but such discrimination would presumably be limited in amount and capable of regulation by general agreement among the members.

The degree of trade liberalization in western Europe is usually measured against the value of non-governmental intra-European imports in 1948. The trade thus freed from quantitative controls was raised by most countries to 75 per cent by the beginning of 1952, and since then a number of countries have gone to 90 per cent or more.

The course of liberalization has seldom run smoothly, and individual countries have had to back-track from time to time in order to deal with a payments crisis. Thus France suspended liberalization completely in February, 1952, while Germany terminated an earlier suspension in January, 1952. The United Kingdom cut liberalized imports from 90 to 61 per cent in November, 1951, reduced them further to 46 per cent in March, 1952, but increased the coverage to 58 per cent in March, 1953, and to 75 per cent in October, 1953.

The OEEC–EPU has come to recognize more and more the importance of domestic financial policies on the trade and payments situation of its members, and has taken an increasing interest in these matters through study and consultation. It has no formal prohibition against considering such matters as does the IMF and the members recognize that their domestic policies often have an external effect. However, it is more difficult to protect the situation from disturbing factors from out-side. The sterling area payments crisis of 1951 was dealt with not only by restrictions against the dollar but also against the Continent. It is clear that the substitution of an EPU balance for balances with the individual members, by introducing at least that degree of multilateralism, has permitted greater lee-way in dealing with trade fluctuations; on external balances it has had less visible effect.

This work by OEEC is usually defended either as a step towards ultimate European economic unity or as a step in correcting the prevailing disequilibrium in world trade. The benefits derived from it in this latter view are in general those flowing from the substitution of limited multilateral trade for still more limited bilateral trade. The presumed advantages are: (a) gains due to increased trade resulting from the relaxa-tion of trade barriers within the group, (b) additional dollar sales because of cost reductions through increased scale of production or competition within Europe and through access to cheaper raw materials, (c) investment patterns more in accord with a fully multilateral world, and (d) greater pres-sure towards monetary and fiscal adjustments within each coun-try. These advantages have not been fully realized because quantitative restrictions were frequently not relaxed where established interests in a country could prevent it and because the creation of a preferential area tended to make sales within the area somewhat easier than dollar sales. To some extent, trade was diverted rather than created.

It is difficult to evaluate the argument in support of efforts to reduce barriers to intra-European trade that competition within the area will therefore be increased, that this will lead to increased efficiency, and that this will act as a force to strengthen European sales in markets outside the European area. This seems to be a series of propositions with many leak-ages in it, so that the premise does not necessarily lead assuredly to the proposed conclusion. On the contrary, it is quite easy to postulate that a preferred market in Europe may reduce some of the pressure to venture into other areas, or to argue that competition is a state of mind and not much more likely to be developed in a large area than a small one. Despite these caveats, most analysts would agree that removing barriers will tend to lower rather than increase costs. It is clear that the EPU made possible a considerable expansion in intra-European trade and this is certainly to be desired.

It is interesting to note that there was little or no liberalization in agriculture. It is not within the power of an international organization to induce countries to pursue policies in opposition to strong domestic pressure.

The basic issue which appears is whether or not such a regional preference system works against the achieving of an even wider multilateralism. Obviously, if the result were to raise barriers against the rest of the world and to lower them within the area, many would question such a step. But the situation has been one of lowering barriers within the area while keeping the outside barriers unchanged—how should that be regarded? Certainly the advantages listed above are important, yet it means the establishment of new patterns which probably still do not represent the best allocation of resources within a yet wider area.

Nor is the assurance that barriers will not be raised against outside areas always easy to maintain. How can one judge the action of the United Kingdom in 1951 when it increased restrictions against both the United States and the EPU area? Also there is the illustration of Belgium when it had for some time been a persistent creditor in EPU to a point in excess of its quota. The program which was suggested, and which was followed for a while, was that Belgium should place additional restrictions against the importation of United States goods as a means of encouraging purchasing power to flow to European supplies and thus help to correct her intra-European payments position. The good neighbor policy within the European economy came into direct conflict with that of a good neighbor in the world economy. The choice for Belgium was that of discriminating against the United States in order to enjoy discrimination in her favor by the other members of EPU.

What would have happened in the absence of EPU–OEEC? It is conceivable that the pressure to make monetary and structural adjustments would have been greater and they would have been made more rapidly, and that some of the countries might have become able to have convertible currencies. This is of course highly speculative. It is difficult to envisage the problems which this might have created for some countries like France. It is possible, but a little unlikely, that Holland would have taken measures sooner to get into balance. It is doubtful whether other countries would have had the courage to liberalize without the added resources that OEEC provided to handle the problems during the period of adjustment. Certainly few countries outside OEEC have achieved convertibility and some are further away from it than in 1946.

The importance of the EPU in the monetary field will be discussed later along with the important question of what functions would remain to it in a world of convertibility. So far as trade liberalization is concerned, its great function has been to provide a reciprocal basis for removing quantitative restrictions among its members. This purpose has not yet been completely achieved, so there remains a not unimportant task to be done. There still remain also the quantitative restrictions against countries outside the area as well as tariff barriers, but these fall in the province of GATT.

The Schuman Plan

A different type of experiment in trade liberalization is that of the European Coal and Steel Community. The Schuman Plan aims at establishing a common market for coal and steel within the six member countries, eliminating national discrimination. It proposes to eliminate various barriers to the free movement of coal and steel erected by national governments on the one hand and to guard against the danger of cartels (relating to activities within the area) on the other. It proposes to seek lower costs and to provide for efficient expansion. In a sense, it treats national governments and cartels as rival claimants to a sovereignty which it seeks to transfer to the High Authority.

In the minds of its originators, the Plan probably was more important as part of a strategy to unite Europe than as a device to increase the efficiency of the European steel and coal industries. The problem of Franco-German relations was uppermost, rather than that of the two industries, and what was envisaged was a progressive entanglement of the economies of the member countries until control over those economies could no longer be exercised effectively by any one of them and sovereignty would quietly pass to the High Authority. Thus the Coal and Steel Community under the compulsions to which it will give rise must eventually become the prototype for similar arrangements in other sectors; or, if this does not happen, national differences will get the upper hand and it either will operate increasingly like an international cartel or will disappear.

In general, the Plan involves an abrogation of national control within national markets for coal and steel and the transfer of those powers to the High Authority, with stated safeguards over that exercise. The High Authority, however, has no control over wage, monetary, fiscal, and other policies controlling the demand for coal and steel or their costs of production, although these policies may have a greater impact on the two industries than any measures that the Authority is free to take on its own initiative. The wage levels in one country, for example, may have important repercussions on the competitive position of that country's coal and steel industries.

Thus either the plan is to be regarded as a step towards European federation or as a series of technical arrangements of little outstanding importance. If there is no further move toward federation, any crisis that arises will be found to originate in elements outside the control of the High Authority. There may then arise a sense of frustration, a re-emergence of nationalist sentiment, and a collapse of the impulse toward unity.

There are various ways of judging after, say five years, the

success of the High Authority. One might examine the trend
in productivity and the change in the conditions of those who
earn their living in the two industries. Or one might list the
frequency with which an emergency has been declared, maximum prices fixed, and so on, although this is perhaps a test
of the economic climate and of the policies of governments
rather than of the success of the High Authority. One might
also study the magnitude of the change in the channels of trade,
the degree to which a selective expansion or contraction has
occurred among countries. The number of high-cost plants
shut down is perhaps one test of this; the elimination of cross-
hauls is another, although in some circumstances cross-hauls
may be a symptom of active competition. It is unlikely, indeed
impossible, where industries have already been nationalized,
that anything like free competition will emerge. But there
should certainly be more competition in services and quality
and perhaps even in price, not only within each country but
across national boundaries.

It may be argued that the best criterion, given the gradiant
of real income and hence a growing consumption of coal and
steel, is whether the growing points of production are in low
cost or high cost areas. The pattern of new investment is the
ultimate test on this basis and the problem which the Authority
will face is to decide in advance on relative costs in ignorance
of some of the important relevant factors (notably raw material prices and exchange rates) and at the risk of choosing
the wrong factors and disregarding those that really matter.

That changes will occur in the new situation is already
evident. For example, (a) the Belgian coal industry is generally
thought to be relatively inefficient. The Belgians have, therefore, been given power to insulate their market by maintaining
restrictions (subject to approval by the High Authority) which
will prevent a fall in output faster than 3 per cent per annum.
(b) The finishing sections of the French steel industry are
thought to be inefficient because there are large numbers of
small fabricating units widely scattered so that trans-shipment
and reheating are necessary. Somehow, concentration of those

plants will be necessary. (c) The south German market is at present supplied largely from the Ruhr because of the structure of rail freights. The Germans have brought down freights so as to put French suppliers on an equal footing (at some sacrifice in rail revenue) and this should increase competition. On the other hand, the Austrian industry feels itself in danger of exclusion from the south German market.

Another problem resembles that suggested by the discussion of EPU. The interests of outside countries may suffer through the creation of what is, in effect, a preferential system of trade. There have been discussions of this danger at GATT and OEEC, the High Authority seeking to be treated at GATT as virtually a separate national entity and so escape the charge of discrimination. Similarly at OEEC the six member countries are open to the charge of removing quantitative restrictions in a discriminatory manner, contrary to the Code of Liberalization. At OEEC, the High Authority gave an assurance that it would deal equitably with the requirements of other members of the OEEC but could make no commitment on this. Allocation of scarce grades of coal are made currently by OEEC in association with the Economic Commission for Europe, but the High Authority has not elected to declare a state of shortage for coal since only a few grades are scarce (e. g., cooking coal and anthracite). Only after such a declaration could it fix export quotas from its member countries.

The Schuman Plan is an interesting intermediate point, between the pulls of nationalism and integration, in international arrangements. It seems evident that whether such a partial unification is workable will depend in large part on whether the participating countries tend to converge or diverge in their separate national policies in matters such as taxes, wages, etc. If the divergence is great, there will be grave difficulty in achieving a single market in this one segment of the six economies. Of course, if other areas of economic or other activity are brought under a single authority, for example, the European Defense Community, this will brighten the prospects for success.

United States Policy

An additional area of trade liberalization calling for special comment is the United States of America. Whereas commodity imports into the United States averaged about $2.5 billions in 1936–38, the total was $11.0 billions in 1951 and $10.7 billions in 1952. In 1952, imports by volume were 51 per cent above prewar. During this same period, tariffs were substantially reduced by trade agreement negotiation, to which must be added the effect of higher valuations in reducing the effectiveness of specific duties (those defined as so many cents per dozen or pound). Nevertheless, there still remains a substantial tariff barrier. The Bell Report summarizes the present situation as follows:

" It is sometimes claimed that United States tariffs are of no importance because 55 per cent of United States imports are duty free and the ratio of duties collected to the value of dutiable imports is only 12.5 per cent. This ratio is misleading because a major share of imports into this country are raw materials and foodstuffs not produced here and on which there is no duty at all. The very high duties on many manufactures which limit severely or exclude entirely their importation are also unreflected in the ratio. Neither are the quotas which set positive limits on the imports of certain agricultural goods. The reduction of tariffs under the Reciprocal Trade Agreements program has made it possible for imports to compete in the American market only to a limited extent." [1]

Much of the tariff reduction under the Reciprocal Trade Agreements program may well have been more apparent than real in that there was excessive protection to start with and, even after reduction, the tariffs may have been high enough to afford ample protection. The United States market for a rather long period has been substantially protected by economic conditions rather than trade barriers as a result of the depression,

[1] The Public Advisory Board for Mutual Security, *A Trade and Tariff Policy in the National Interest* (Washington, 1953), 4.

the war, and the postwar shortage period. Certainly, there was little impact of the tariff reductions prior to 1949, if one uses escape clause applications as a measure. However, as to tariff barriers themselves, a recent tabulation prepared at the Fletcher School of Law and Diplomacy (not covering the entire tariff list) noted 138 items for which the tariff rates are over 60 per cent on an ad valorem basis.

How much promise does further tariff reduction by the United States have in contributing to the objective of increasing trade? To what extent may we expect that foreign countries would be able to increase their dollar earnings? Unfortunately, there are various reasons for not being comfortably optimistic about achieving an extensive increase in imports into the United States, even if there were a definite national policy so to do.

One approach is to examine the relationship that has prevailed historically between United States commodity imports and national income. This relationship appears to have been remarkably constant over long periods of time except for two downward breaks in the ratio (1898 and 1938), irrespective of changes in the structure or level of United States tariffs. Fluctuations in imports seem to be closely related to United States domestic activity, and such shifts as have occurred have been to a lower basis at times not related to tariff changes. One explanation of the failure of the ratio to change relates to the large part that agricultural products play in United States imports. Since the United States resources displaced by increased agricultural imports tend to remain in the agricultural sector, they tend to be shifted to the production of other import-competing and income-absorbing agricultural items. This, in turn, is conducive to a decrease in the importation of some other agricultural products. This same sort of substitution may take place in connection with other types of commodities. (This analysis seems to disregard the possibility that an import may also cause a complementary demand.) As for the future, any increase in United States imports of leather, rubber, silk, and fats and oils bids fair to be limited by the growing use of domestically made synthetics and substitutes. Technological developments which make possible great economies in the use of certain metals, such as the electrolytic process in the use of tin for galvanizing, should also offset to some degree the various forecasts which anticipate fast-growing imports of metals and minerals over the next twenty-five years.

Difficulties of increasing imports are also to be found on the supply side. In many cases, foreign producers of presently protected items are not in a position to increase quickly their output of goods that could be sold in the United States. Not only is there the problem of the availability of capital and appropriate skills of labor and management required to increase output, but there is also the time factor for expansion and tooling. Equally important would be the time required to arrange in the United States for proper distribution facilities. Of course, if the goods were now flowing into third markets, a diversion to the United States market would not be a production problem but the marketing problems would still remain.

The degree to which foreign producers could and would take advantage of reduced barriers to the American market is clearly conjecture but at least two estimates are available. The Bell Report presented a program for modifying various laws and regulations governing trade and estimated that such changes would increase imports after an interval of three years or more, by $700 millions to $1 billion, of which $500–$700 millions would be an increase in the imports of manufactures.[2] An analysis by Piquet[3] of the possible effect of removal of United States tariff barriers based on 1951 trade data concluded that the temporary suspension of all tariffs and quotas might lead after a three to five year period to an import increase of between $1.2 and $2.6 billions per year. If tariffs alone were to be suspended, the estimated increase of imports might amount to between $800 millions and $1.8 billions. Probably

[2] The Public Advisory Board for Mutual Security, *A Trade and Tariff Policy In the National Interest* (Washington, 1953), 5.

[3] Howard S. Piquet, *Aid, Trade and the Tariff* (New York, 1953).

more than 40 per cent of the dutiable commodities that now
enter the United States would not be noticeably affected by
tariff suspension. The imports that would probably cause an
appreciable displacement of domestic manufactures because of
inelastic or contracting demand are estimated to amount to
about $860 millions. They would affect about thirty different
lines of production, the value of whose domestic output
amounted to slightly less than $4 billions in 1951.

According to Piquet, of the countries that faced balance-
of-payments difficulties in 1951, the principal beneficiaries from
the suspension of United States import restrictions would be
the United Kingdom, France, West Germany, Denmark, and
Italy. Cuba and Canada, which had not experienced such difficulties in 1951, would also be greatly benefited. Indeed, if
tariffs alone were to be suspended, it appears that imports from
countries not receiving American aid would increase by about
the same extent as imports from countries that did receive aid,
while quota suspension would benefit non-recipients of aid
more than recipients.

There are a number of questions which arise if one attempts
to estimate the quantitative effects of tariff and quota suspension on United States imports. Any estimate must necessarily
be subject to a series of biases. The assumption (made by
Piquet) that there would be no change in United States import
prices after tariff removal may give the estimates an upward
bias. It is by no means obvious as to what the effects of tariff
cuts might be on internal prices or how any reduction in the
government take might be distributed among foreign manufacturers, foreign exporters, domestic importers, and consumers.
Certainly it cannot be obtained in full by all four. If the
domestic price falls, for example, by only part of the tariff cut,
the existing foreign manufacturer or importer would gain an
unexpected differential which he might take as added profit or
which might lead him into increasing his offering in the market.
Or the lower price might drive some marginal domestic producer out of the market, permitting some foreign producer to
replace him on the supply schedule. It is very likely that

United States import prices would fall to some point between prevailing prices and such prices minus the tariffs. In other words, calculations based on unchanging prices tend to overstate the extent to which the dollar receipts of foreigners would be increased.

In contrast, to the extent that the figures do not take account of new products which might enter the United States market, a downward bias is introduced. Moreover, it is impossible to know what allowances to make for how far given imports may be either competitive or complementary with each other, i. e., to what extent an increase in imports of one item might cause either an increase or a decrease in the imports of other items. It also should be noted, in thinking about balance-of-payments effects, that an increase of certain types of imports into the United States may result in burdens on other countries from which such imports may be diverted. Thus, the diversion of an item like Italian or Spanish olive oil from western Europe to the United States may result in an increased cost of olive oil to western Europe.

The authors of the estimates cited earlier would be the first to insist that they have merely done the best they could to quantify the problem and that a wide margin of error necessarily exists. But whatever the extent by which imports would be increased, at least the situation would be improved, subject to the various comments made in Chapter II concerning the relationship of trade to aid.

The fact that the impact of even a substantial tariff reduction on the economy as a whole would be small in magnitude (probably only a small fraction of 1 per cent of our total national consumption) does not mean that no one would be injured by such a drastic step as the suspension of the tariff. Certain individuals and establishments would be hurt, but their number undoubtedly would be small. One estimate places the number of workers who might be affected by removal of tariffs and quotas at approximately 200,000. The more modest program in the Bell Report estimates that imports of manufactures would displace the output of 60,000 to 90,000

workers but that the actual displacement would probably be
less than 45,000. Such an adjustment is extremely small compared with the over-all adjustments which are continually
taking place in our economy as the result of new products,
technology, shifting styles, relocation of plants, deaths, and
retirement turnover.

The fact is that United States population and United States
markets are growing. Part of the increase in imports could
provide for this increasing demand, thereby permitting many
domestic industries at least to hold their own. Moreover, it is
quite probable that the profit margins of many firms which
might be affected by increased imports are such as to permit
the absorption of the lower competitive prices that might
accompany increased foreign competition. Even if certain
enterprises were forced to curtail or stop production of given
products due to increased foreign competition, this in itself
would not necessarily mean serious injury, since many of them
produce more than one commodity and therefore have a number of available avenues of adjustment. (Garlic growers seldom
have 10 per cent of their acreage in that particular crop.)

If United States tariffs were lowered on a slow and gradual
basis as recommended, for example, by the Bell Report and
by the French Plan at GATT, the displacement of workers
and capital could take place at a rate which would be related
to turnover and growth and would keep the difficulties of
readjustment at a minimum. Such gradual declines would also
give marginal producers the necessary time to adjust themselves
to the new market conditions through the adoption of more
efficient and lower cost methods of production.

Despite the advantages inherent in a gradual lowering of
United States tariffs, certain political considerations might make
a single and definitive action more desirable. The mere fact
that gradual decreases must necessarily extend over a number
of years gives a continuous opportunity to advocates of protection to press for a cessation of the scheduled reductions and
preservation of what protection remains. In contrast, if it
became possible to reduce greatly or remove tariffs by a single

stroke, there would be little protection left to be saved. Attempts to restore tariff barriers once they have been removed would be more difficult than attempts merely to maintain them against further reductions. In any event, there appears to be some justification for the assumption that even a marked reduction of tariffs would have very little immediate effect on domestic producers. Foreign imports would only build up slowly in response to a tariff cut—the full effects might not be felt for somewhere between five and ten years.

During the last twenty years, such tariff reductions as have been made have followed the principle of reciprocity. In negotiating trade agreements, the effort has been made to equalize the value of trade for which concessions are made with that for which concessions are obtained. The Reciprocal Trade Agreements Act was a product of the depression when concern was not so much over equilibrium as over the depressed level of "two-way trade." Obviously, if concern today is to increase foreign earnings, the concept of reciprocity seems not to be particularly appropriate and unilateral United States reduction, to the extent that imports might increase, would presumably be reflected in some beneficial way in the American balance of payments. The great advantage of unilateral action is that it can be taken without any external complications (assuming it involves lowering the tariff, of course).

There are some who feel that while the United States tariff should be lowered, the United States should make use of the bargaining value of tariff reduction so far as possible. This might mean continuing the policy of reciprocal bargaining on the general theory that any restriction is a bad restriction and the more the barriers can be removed the better. Our action might be conditional upon other countries, say the Europeans, making tariff cuts not on goods for which the United States is the principal market but on goods important in intra-European or third country trade, thus improving the multilateral possibility of trade. There are several possible compromises between the unilateral and reciprocal position and it is possible to have some of both. Perhaps the most important notion is that the executive branch not be limited in its action to pursuing reciprocity exclusively, since unilateral tariff reduction by the United States would be better than no reduction at all.

Many different formulae have been suggested for lowering the American tariff—by various categories or across the board, by reducing all duties by a given percentage, or by reducing all above 50 per cent to that figure and all below that to the next lowest multiple of ten, etc. Another approach would make a single cut in tariffs but limit by an increasing quota the consequential imports over a fixed period. While those interested in particular commodities are, of course, greatly concerned about the formula used, the public interest lies rather in generally increasing imports by whatever formula.

One suggestion recently put forward is that whenever the free imports of any commodity equal a fixed percentage of the United States production of that commodity, the full duty would become applicable, 10 per cent of United States production being cited as a possible figure. Such a formula appears simple and concrete, might prove to be politically acceptable, and might furnish the type of incentive to deficit countries that seemingly less drastic tariff reduction under the Reciprocal Trade Agreements Program does not afford.

The operation of a proposal of this sort involves certain administrative difficulties. Among them is the problem of defining an industry or a product. Thus, if a volume of shoes valued at 10 per cent of United States production were permitted to come in free and they all entered in the form of sport shoes, such imports could cause havoc in the sport branch of the shoe industry. Difficulties would also arise in regard to the distribution of the free segment of imports among importers. If present imports of a given commodity aggregated 15 per cent of total production, who should be permitted the first 10 per cent that would be brought in free of tariffs? Should the principle of " first come—first served " be followed, or should licenses be granted to importers on an historical basis, or should tariff-free licenses be auctioned? Or should there be a system of tariff refunds which would be apportioned among all importers; that is, if imports total 15 per cent of production, each importer would receive a rebate of ten-fifteenths of the duty paid?

It should also be noted that any plan for tariff removal that was applicable to, for example, 10 per cent of domestic production might have little or no direct effect on the volume of foreign sales of those goods which are already being brought into the United States in excess of that amount. In such cases the suspension of the tariff on a fraction of the imports might really turn out to be merely a windfall to certain importers. There is the further danger that a percentage limitation upon free imports might lead to furthering the use of the quota concept in United States tariff policy. The idea of 10 per cent of domestic production might come to be considered the foreigners' " fair share " of the market and hence tend to become the maximum.

With respect to any action which is taken in the tariff field, it is important that it be firm and that it not include the type of uncertainty created by the present escape-clause provisions. It seems to be generally agreed that one of the most powerful barriers to the further development of imports is not so much the existing tariff and quota provisions as the uncertainty among foreign exporters as to United States tariff rates in the future. In the cheese quota case, it was evident that considerable investment had been made by foreign producers in packaging and processing to American taste, not to mention the development of distribution arrangements. Such investment is not likely to be made if the foreign exporter is worried that United States tariffs will be raised once the United States market has been successfully entered.

The above discussion has dealt with the problem of tariffs and quotas. It should at least be mentioned that there are various other points where changes in laws or regulations might encourage increased dollar earnings. For example, the removal of " Buy American " requirements from certain United States legislation might increase imports appreciably. The simplification and standardization of tariff administrative procedures, particularly as they affect methods of classification and valuation, would also be a significant factor in stimulating imports. And the shipping field is another where other countries might be permitted to earn more dollars, if certain of the requirements with respect to the division of cargo were modified.

After all is said and done, the case for a reduction in the United States tariff rests only in part on economic grounds. It would probably add directly to the economic welfare of the United States only in a limited degree. It would help the farmer and the export industries and the foreign investor while increasing competition for certain domestic manufacturing industries. It might help the taxpayer and the consumer somewhat. But foreign trade is a minor factor in the total United States economy in the short run, at any rate. The more important issue is whether a substantial reduction in barriers may not be desirable, unilaterally or otherwise, in the interests of an expanding world economy and of a continuing Western Alliance.

Stabilizing the Terms of Trade

Still a different concern over reducing international trade difficulties has appeared in connection with the terms of trade, particularly as they reflect differences in behavior between raw materials and manufactured products. Representatives of countries which are chiefly producers of primary products contend that their terms of trade have been undergoing secular deterioration and intolerable cyclical fluctuations. This condition creates wide fluctuations in their foreign earnings, particularly in those cases where one or two raw materials dominate a country's exports, while their imports, covering the gamut of capital goods, manufactured consumers' goods, and food, are more stable in cost to them.

One can be skeptical concerning the validity of the secular forecast (as discussed in the previous chapter), but there is no doubt about the fact that short-term swings in raw materials usually have the greatest amplitude in the price spectrum. Nor is the problem only one of price. A report by the United

Nations shows that cyclical swings in volume are as wide as those of price and in the same direction. It might be that a more stable price condition would increase the fluctuations in volume, or vice versa.

This short-term instability of primary material prices and volumes has an adverse effect both on the underdeveloped countries which produce such commodities and on the rest of the world. Wide price fluctuations hinder the continuous maintenance of a regular flow of trade. The severity and suddenness in the changes in their terms of trade do not allow raw-materials producing countries time to shift the use of their resources to compensate for such changes even if they could. The result has been a tendency by such countries to impose restrictions on imports in bad years, and they never seem to be entirely dismantled in good years. Nevertheless, the good years see great increases in foreign orders placed which carry over to accentuate the difficulty of any new and sudden downward change in their fortunes.

These wide fluctuations make the possibility of sustained profits more uncertain, and it is thought that consequently they discourage investment in these fields. The investor in exploring for new sources of raw materials faces a double risk. Not only is there the risk of failure to find the materials he is looking for in sufficient quantities to make exploitation profitable, but even if he does find them, the wide fluctuations in their market position may make the development of the discovered materials highly speculative (unless it fits into a vertically integrated enterprise which can assure a market). In spite of this argument, the net effect of fluctuations in raw material prices on investment in the exploitation of new resources is not clear. Indeed, it may be that the increased investment stimulated by periods of great profitability (since no one can be sure as to how long they will last) may result in a greater total investment over a long period than would have taken place if raw material prices had been stable. At any rate, since imports, exports, and the terms of trade in such countries are important determinants of national income, saving, capital formation,

monetary stability, and government revenues, erratic and un-
predictable changes in the trade picture make it difficult for
them to plan for their essential requirements and carry out
programs for their development on a sustained basis.

It would be misleading to describe this problem as one
located somehow in the underdeveloped countries. It is often
very important to them, but raw material producers are found
in other countries as well. The drive for an international
stabilization arrangement may come from these producers without much regard for its stabilizing or other effects on the
country as a whole, or on consumers domestic and foreign. In
such cases, it is not merely stability, but stability at a profitable
level which is sought. The producers may succeed, either
publicly or privately, in establishing stabilizing devices by
means of restricting output, allocating markets, or maintaining
prices.

As a basic proposal for the country dependent on a few
primary products, one can suggest diversification, but this is
not without its problems (see Chapter VIII). The most important operation in the stabilization field in the postwar picture is the International Wheat Agreement, which provides a
price floor and price ceiling for both importers and exporters
with respect to predetermined quantities of wheat purchases
and sales. The recently negotiated International Sugar Agreement, when set alongside the United States sugar legislation,
is another example of stabilization (an arrangement which
successfully protects certain high cost producers).

Also various international study groups for specific commodities like cotton, rubber, and tin meet from time to time,
exchange information, and discuss possible plans for stabilization. There are special producer arrangements for some
commodities like tea and cocoa, and other cases where from
time to time individual countries have been in a sufficiently
important position in the world supply picture to take steps
to support prices—Brazil in coffee, Chile in copper, and Australia in wool. The International Materials Conference, set up
when shortages and sky-rocketing raw material prices developed

in 1950, provided a means of assembling data and recommending action to individual governments to ease the disorderly scramble and provide a better international distribution of scarce materials.

The problem might be reduced by ironing out fluctuations in the rate of buying either through long-term contracts or the appropriate handling of inventories. Long-term contracts provide stability for their own coverage (if they are lived up to), but they also freeze the situation so far as trade is concerned and may even accentuate the swings in the remainder of the market. Of course the situation might be eased if the principal consumers would deliberately undertake to bring greater stability into their demand for such materials. Under prevailing practices the consuming countries, in effect, vary their holding of inventories, and this is one of the conditions compounding the effect of declines on raw material producers. The anti-cyclical administration of inventories by building up stock piles or through other devices could lessen the magnitude of price changes and assure more stable incomes to producing countries. This might, of course, be done by an international agency. The chief question which must be raised is whether or not such an agency can be wiser than market speculators or whether its funds will be so unlimited that it need not be specially wise. It is somehow easier for those operating a stabilizing enterprise to buy than to sell.

Some feel that significant advantages might also follow from the wider use of international commodity agreements. However, the price swings tolerated by the Wheat Agreement leave wide scope for fluctuation unless they are (as happened in the first period) outside the real market range so that only the floor or ceiling is operative. Such agreements must be based upon some schedule for sharing the supply and demand—the question is on what basis? Would not any such schedule be likely to deter the opening up of new sources of supply even though they were more economical than existing sources, and might it not impede the expansion of demand where such demand is elastic in response to medium-term price movements? It is doubtful whether such agreements could bring about the desired results without the maintenance of buffer stocks either nationally or internationally.

It should be noted that in a limited program there is the possibility of harm to the countries that produce other raw materials not covered by commodity agreements. That is to say, general price relationships among different primary commodities are themselves of great importance. Since some of the underdeveloped countries are fairly large consumers of a variety of imported primary products, agreements that do not cover a number of products might even increase the instability in their terms of trade. There may be something to be said for an omnibus program rather than separate commodity programs developed independently of each other.

It is by no means certain that the chief beneficiaries of efforts to stabilize the prices of primary products would be the underdeveloped countries if some program of stabilization were successful. These countries are themselves consumers of raw materials which they must import, and some of them are net importers of food. The countries that might benefit most might turn out to be countries like Canada, Australia, and Finland which are not underdeveloped in the ordinary sense of the term nor particularly impoverished. It was estimated, for example, that 95 per cent of the pulp, 90 per cent of the sulfur, 70 per cent of the wheat, nearly half of the cotton, and most of the wool that entered into international trade came from developed countries. The industrial countries should also welcome any progress made towards creating more stable and less erratic markets for their products. The tremendous importance of changes in the terms of trade to the balance of payments of the United Kingdom has already been noted, but this is also true of all countries where foreign trade plays an important part in their economic life.

EAST–WEST TRADE

After considering various attempts to free trade of its impediments, it is perhaps appropriate to take a further look at the outstanding case of liberalization in reverse—East-West trade. About 15 per cent of all imports into western Europe before the war came from eastern Europe. (This figure of course disregards entirely intra-western Europe trade.) Part of this trade represented the culmination of Germany's efforts to bring Rumania, Bulgaria, and other eastern European countries within her orbit, and this trade was often conducted at inflated prices. The figures ought properly to be adjusted in order to show the more normal patterns of exchange between East and West; but the deduction can hardly be a large one as not much over one quarter of this total trade was into Western Germany. The reduction in trade that has taken place in the years since the war has already been described in Chapter IV.

The objectives of the Soviet bloc appear to be aimed at self-sufficiency and at linking the satellites more firmly to the Soviet Union. The trade objectives of the West are aimed at preventing the export of commodities of primary strategic significance and limiting the export of commodities of lesser strategic significance. It is essential that in such a situation where normal economic criteria for trade do not apply, that there be substantial uniformity among the various countries. Country A will not stop selling if Country B continues to sell. The broad principle on which there is agreement must be applied in terms of specific transactions. As one might expect, differences in detail appear in large part as the result of differences in economic, geographical, and psychological position.

So far as items with an obvious military potential are concerned there is no dispute—the only possible principle in a cold war must be one of embargo. But military potential is shadowy and there comes a point when it fades into economic potential. It is usual to assume that trade benefits both parties; at what stage should that benefit take precedence over a possible loss of military potential?

There are some who would reply that trade with the East should be carried on as long as more is received than is traded away, that we are too prone to view the problem solely in terms of what we send and not in terms of what we take away. Such a position if taken literally would mean no interference at all with private trade. Clearly, the calculus to be applied must be different from that of maximum economic advantage and closer to the calculus used by the mercantilists in the days when cold war was treated as normal. It must take account not only of the advantages to the West but also of any countervailing advantage to the East. It must have regard to relative economic strength and to the comparative advantage of the trade to the other side.

This principle, too, if carried to its logical conclusion (and if one had the information to make the necessary judgments), would tend to have extreme consequences. If adopted by both sides, it would inevitably bring trade virtually to a standstill. It is obviously the correct principle when countries are already at war, but is perhaps too demanding in the standard which it sets up for cold war conditions.

In any event, it is important to keep in mind that the trade is not large, that there is a common effort to embargo strategic items, and that probably even without any restrictions the trade would not have been much greater. There are some who think it would be sensible to attempt to maximize trade in consumers goods (i. e., Palestine oranges for Soviet Union oil). On the other hand, others are concerned with the development of any dependence on the East. They regard the swift effectiveness of the embargo against Yugoslavia as a warning. Perhaps these points of view can be reconciled by continuing to develop alternative sources of supplies and alternative markets, while encouraging some degree of trade in " peaceful " products. However, this problem is clearly less one of economics than of political and human relations—relations with the East and relations within the West.

CHAPTER VI

The Levels of Foreign Exchange Rates

FOREIGN exchange rates express the rate at which one currency may be exchanged for another. In terms of international economic arrangements, it is the connecting link between the price levels of two countries or of one country and the rest of the world, and therefore is an important factor in encouraging or discouraging exports or imports as well as influencing other items in the balance of payments such as tourism and investment.

In the nineteenth century, exchange rates were fixed by the fact that currencies could be converted into gold and gold could be used as payment. Therefore, the exchange rate approximated the relative gold content of the currencies and did not fluctuate beyond the costs of gold shipment. The system of unrestricted currency interchangeability at fixed rates existed until 1914 and for a few years in the 1920's.

It came to an end with the introduction of foreign exchange controls in many countries, beginning in central Europe in 1931. The depression years before the second World War were marked by a series of more or less competitive and retaliatory exchange depreciations in the attempt to protect reserves and export unemployment, with Germany in particular demonstrating that exchange machinery might be used as a foreign policy instrument.

FIXED EXCHANGE RATES

During the war and immediately thereafter, a good deal of thinking, planning, and negotiating was devoted to the purpose of establishing sound and satisfactory monetary relations. As has already been noted, instead of concentrating on the immediate task of how to restore a balanced trade and payments picture and an international system of settlements, it was assumed that this would somehow come about, and the planning concentrated largely on drawing up the blueprint and obtaining policy agreement for operations in the world after a transition period of perhaps five years.

During this transition period, the new world rules would not apply except those relating to the fixing of par values, which were applied immediately. Article 14 (Articles of Agreement of the International Monetary Fund) recognized nearly unlimited rights during the interim period for each country to " maintain and adapt to changing circumstances restrictions on payments and transfers for current international transactions." The lack of any further directives for this transitional period put little check on the development of bilateralism, discrimination, and elaborate control machinery.

The drafters were clearly impressed by the experience of the prewar years with their predominantly deflationary pressures and exchange depreciations. They therefore regarded the maintenance of fixed exchange rates as a matter of great importance. They did not anticipate that the pressures of the postwar years were to be inflationary and that tendencies towards a tenacious clinging to established exchange rates might become increasingly inappropriate as inflationary pressures were to assert themselves. Thus, the Articles of Agreement were more concerned with the definition of par values and the maintenance of stable exchange rates than with the establishment of free exchange markets or of multilateral payments systems free from bilateralism and unnecessary discriminations.

The emphasis therefore was on establishing and maintaining fixed exchange rates. In ideal conditions, the virtues of fixed rates are obvious. Stable money is important to any economy, and foreign exchange is the money of the international world. It is frequently necessary to enter into long-term financial commitments covering a transaction between citizens of two countries. The terms of any long-term contract are most equitably fulfilled when the values of the two currencies concerned are constant and the exchange rate between them is also constant.

In a world in which these ideal conditions seldom prevail, it appears to be generally desirable on grounds of equity that the exchange rate shall be constant or at least capable of having fluctuations offset in a futures market. However, if the two economies involved have quite different price trends, then the fixed rate may be inequitable. In such a case, it is not impossible that a movement of an exchange rate which reflects the movement of relative costs and prices in the two countries might yield a more, and not less, equitable settlement of the contract.

But most of the arguments for a fixed rate are of a more technical character. When an exchange rate has been ruling for some period, it will have the effect of creating an adaptation to itself, either by an increase in exports and a reduction in imports, or *vice versa*. Such an adaptation may take an appreciable time to be accomplished. It is desirable to stabilize the rate for a sufficient period to produce these effects, more particularly if elasticities of supply and demand are low for the short run so that otherwise there is a risk of unstable equilibrium.

Furthermore, if a suitable rate can be fixed and held with sufficient strength to ensure that there is a general belief that the rate can continue to be held, short-term speculation will usually help to maintain the stability of the rate—a fall in the quotation within the limits allowed by the fixed rate will lead business men who have future payments to make, and speculators who expect that there will later be a countervailing demand for the currency, to buy now. In the nineteenth century it was always assumed that stabilizing speculation would normally support any gold standard currency which momentarily fell below its par value. In the case of a fluctuating rate, speculation is probably more likely to be perverse, unless it is assumed that an equalization fund will support a currency at certain points and thus in effect give it many of the qualities of a fixed exchange. That is to say, if the currency shows signs of weakening, speculators (and indeed many who have payments to make in the currency) will assume a further fall in the fluctuating rate and will hold off buying and thus contribute to the fall.

The above argument is only valid if it is believed that the fixed rate can in fact be held. If there is widespread doubt, as there has been on a number of occasions in recent years, as to whether the currency is not overvalued and as to whether the authorities managing the currency concerned have in fact sufficient reserves or are willing to take other steps to maintain the existing fixed rate, speculation may easily become perverse for a fixed rate and build up with added intensity because, if the rate breaks, it will probably lead to a devaluation large enough to yield big profits to those who have anticipated it.

A further advantage of a fixed rate is that, in the case of a country which depends heavily on imported foodstuffs and materials so that the price of imports is very closely reflected in the cost of living, a fixed rate is rather less likely to generate a spiral of rising prices, wages, costs, and again prices. This case can be generalized more widely. If the necessary adjustment in the exchange rate would increase the price of imports, and this increase in the price of imports would increase the cost of living, and this increase in the cost of living would lead to higher wage rates, the final result might be a rise in domestic prices which would offset the exchange rate adjustment and would still leave the basic disequilibrium untouched. Such a situation denies adjustment since it assumes fixed relationships among the parts where adjustment must be made. Certainly much of this inflexibility does exist, although there are other monetary and fiscal weapons in the hands of governments if they will use them.

The arguments in favor of the fixed rate require the assumption that the rate is fairly reasonable. The more it is out of line, the more some action in another field will be required to maintain it. A government may support an exchange rate by entering the market itself and using resources or borrowing additional resources if it feels that the pressure is temporary. It may endeavor to deal with the problem by import restrictions or payments controls. These restrictions may prohibit unlicensed payments to foreign countries, unlicensed imports of goods and services, unlicensed loans to non-residents, exports not paid for in foreign currency surrendered to the monetary authorities, exports priced below a value acceptable to the authorities, payments of service on foreign investment, etc. Finally, the government may support the rate by taking domestic action such as tightening credit or even encouraging structural adjustment. Of course, there may be many other reasons why a government may consider it necessary to impose controls of one sort or another, but the maintenance of a fixed exchange rate which, having gotten " out of line," calls for restrictions which tend to perpetuate a fundamental disequilibrium, has little that can be said in its defense.

Still there are some who feel that there are various circumstances where it is better not to rely upon the exchange rate to be the rationer of foreign purchasing power. For example, in the immediate postwar years when there were acute shortages of goods, there were so many interferences and arbitrary allocations like rationing, price control, government purchase, and the like, that the rate of exchange had relatively little effect (except in determining amounts of counterpart funds). But this is reasoning from a set of circumstances which are probably not permanent. Rationing and price controls are slowly disappearing. Furthermore, for many countries where government controls are not administered with full effectiveness and fairness, the influence of the exchange rate for what it may be worth may lead to much better results in economic terms than the process of granting licenses to individual business men. Again, this requires that the rate be somewhere near a proper level.

DEVALUATIONS

There have been more than a hundred currency devaluations since 1945; most currencies have been devalued at least

once, some twice or even more. How can this fact be reconciled
with the statement that governments in recent years have
tended to avoid devaluation and to cling to fixed exchange
rates, however inappropriate, and with the suggestion of a
contrast between a fashion of " competitive exchange devaluation " of the 1930's and a propensity to " defend exchange
stability " after the second World War?

The contrast is a real one. Under the deflationary pressures
of the 1930's governments resorted to devaluation in order to
undervalue their currencies, to " export the unemployment "
from which they were suffering, and to promote the emergence
of higher prices and incomes. Under the inflationary pressures
of the postwar years, governments resorted to devaluation,
usually after long hesitation, in order to correct overvaluations
of their currencies, the inflation of which had resulted in excess
demand for homemade as well as imported goods and to adjust
the prices of foreign monies, especially the more stable dollar,
to already increased prices and incomes.

It should also be noted that exchange rates, which may have
been appropriate in the past, could be too high even with no
price and income changes, due to changes in the international
economic relations of a country. For example, a new rate might
be needed if income from foreign investment were lost, or the
competitive position should deteriorate, or demand for a country's traditional exports should shift, or it found itself with
increased requirements for foreign supplies. It was no easy
thing to determine the appropriate par value in the years immediately after the war.

The effectiveness of a devaluation in improving the situation depends upon many factors. The discussion about the
effects of the 1949 devaluation of the pound sterling and of the
series of devaluations which followed it has not led to generally
accepted conclusions. It is possible to make only short-run
observations about the effect of this set of devaluations on
international trade because of the outbreak of the Korean War
only nine months later. Certainly it is true that the gold and
dollar reserves of the sterling area increased from $1,340 mil-

lions at the time of the devaluation (September, 1949) to $2,422 millions in June, 1950. But this may be attributed in part to "postponed exports" from the sterling countries and postponed payments by their debtors because the devaluation had been anticipated by many, in part to substantially stricter import controls in the sterling area, and in part to an upturn in business activity in the United States.

In spite of the richness of the statistical record, one cannot see clearly the relationship of the devaluation to prices. There are too many forces playing upon price behavior. In the case of primary commodities, prices were influenced by such things as international agreements, national control policies, and fluctuations in the volume of United States imports. Primary prices in the United States held about even while imported manufactured goods fell somewhat in price, although the non-food element in the general wholesale price index was rising. The amount of the decrease for imported manufactured goods varied from product to product, depending upon the elasticities involved, but one estimate places the over-all average decline at about 15 per cent. The trade deficit of the rest of the world with the dollar area fell from $3,321 millions for the first six months of 1949 to $1,150 millions for the first six months of 1950.

But again interpreters refer to increased business activity in the United States, to the stricter restrictions in some countries against imports from the United States, to higher food production in western Europe and other non-dollar areas, to the revival of German industrial production, to reduced shipments under the European Recovery Program, and to other factors besides devaluation which could possibly explain increased shipments to, and reduced shipments from, the United States. Exports to the non-dollar area increased slightly more for the countries which had devalued than those which had not, but the amount of the advantage was small. The devaluing countries did somewhat better in their trade with Canada, chiefly because imports from the United Kingdom were substituted for those from the United States, largely motor cars.

About one-fifth of the improvement was due to increased exports to the dollar area, and the balance was due to reduced purchases from the dollar area. Both the devalued exchange rates and increased restrictions were at work. However, it should be noted that most of the countries employed strict systems of import control prior to devaluation and therefore price changes could hardly have been expected to reduce import demand below the control levels, since presumably some pent-up demand was present behind the trade restrictions. The price increases of imports undoubtedly did help to reduce pressure on the controls and the control authorities. At about this same time, the supply situation was improving in other countries and the fact that supplies were available elsewhere may have been of more importance than the price factor in diverting trade from dollar sources. Probably price was more important with reference to exports to the dollar area where there were few quantitative restrictions against imports. Even here, the fact that the largest increases in American imports were in foodstuffs and raw materials, where the price adjustments were least, would indicate that other factors were more important than price. As for third markets, substitution of western European for United States goods did not appear to be particularly stimulated, but there may not have been time enough before the Korean War dominated the scene.

Devaluation also undoubtedly helped to correct some of the price maladjustments that existed because of the different rates of inflation in different countries during the war and post-war years. One cannot tell whether the extent of devaluation was exactly right everywhere—it may have been excessive in some instances and thus have resulted in undervaluation of currencies and it may have been insufficient in other cases. But there is litle doubt that most of the devaluations had been overdue and did contribute to the general improvement in international conditions which has taken place in more recent years.

Devaluation can have an important influence even when there is a structural inability of a country to increase its output of exportable goods. The price incentives created by devaluation may cause producers (who had not done so under moral suasion) to divert given productive capacity from production for the home market to production for export, or may induce importers to change the source of imports from non-devaluing to devaluing countries, or persuade exporters to change the destination of exports. These shifts may leave total trade volumes unchanged but differently divided between " hard currency " and " soft currency " areas.

A real danger to the ultimate effectiveness of corrective devaluation lies in the necessity of preventing inflationary forces from reasserting themselves. Devaluation may be a useful adjustment after an inflation has been checked, but it will not correct inflationary pressures if they persist and, in fact, may even reinforce them. With unorthodox fiscal policies, easy money policies, and indulgent labor policies, wages, costs, incomes, and prices may soon " catch up " with the new level of foreign exchange rates and may re-establish the disequilibrium. This is the reason why devaluations have often had only transitory effects and why adjusted exchange rates after a while have again been in need of further adjustment.

Among the reasons which create resistance to the process of devaluation on the part of the authorities of a country is that in a sense devaluation is an admission of failure to take various steps to check the inflation which has led to the necessity for an exchange rate adjustment. What gains are made must be preserved by other steps, frequently no different in general type from those needed in the first place. There is a real difference in degree between the problems of checking an inflation and carrying out a deflation, but there is always the danger that the pressures which made the devaluation necessary may again make themselves felt. And of course, if devaluations occur too often, they undermine confidence in the currency and affect the holding of balances and the flow of capital.

MULTIPLE EXCHANGE RATES

There are other ways of altering the exchange rate short of complete devaluation. Among the new inventions of the last twenty-five years is the device of "multiple exchange rates," which since the war has been practiced by at least twenty countries, including twelve Latin American republics. Some of these systems are extremely complicated. In a sense, this technique permits a kind of partial devaluation. It is also a substitute for differential trade restrictions.

A few distinctions may be useful. There are several types of two-rate or multiple-rate systems that do not really belong in the category under discussion: (1) there is the customary differential between a buying rate and a selling rate for foreign exchange quoted by monetary authorities, a practice which had its origin in the two gold points under the gold standard; (2) there are the varying discounts for blocked balances and clearing accounts under exchange controls, discounts that depend on how solidly the accounts are frozen and how easily they can be unfrozen, that is, used for specified purposes and transferred to third persons; (3) there is a black-market rate for almost every currency subject to exchange controls, with the black-market rate differing from the official rate according to the relative size of the demand for foreign exchange that is left unsatisfied by the control authorities, the supply that can escape the official controls, and the penalty, if any, for getting caught; (4) there is the free-market rate in countries that have exchange controls but permit certain exchange transactions to be carried on in a free market at rates according to supply and demand, which may differ from the official rate. The last of these cases may become one of informal devaluation if the transactions that can legally be made at the free-market rate include a large part of the foreign trade of the country concerned.

None of these cases is referred to when one speaks of multiple-rate systems. Multiple-rate systems in use vary in complexity and in purpose. They involve the setting of at least two or more official buying rates for foreign exchange, two or

more official selling rates, or both. In addition, there may be a
free market for certain types of exchange transactions.

Such a system may be used for many purposes. It may be
used to provide revenue by setting low buying rates for the
exchange earned by certain products. It may be used to influence the operation of the economy by increasing or diminishing
returns among exporters, importers, producers, and traders of
particular products or services. It may be used to adjust the
balance of payments.

The attractiveness of a multiple-rate system to underdeveloped countries extends far beyond the field of exchange
rates, exchange restrictions, and balance-of-payments policies.
In such countries, where foreign trade is usually of major importance and where there frequently is not a very highly
developed and effective fiscal and administrative machinery,
the exchange rate machinery may be the most effective instrument at hand for many aspects of economic policy in general.
What another country would do through taxation, subsidies,
rationing, price policy, investment screening, stabilization programs and the like, tends to be done, or can only be achieved
effectively at this stage, through the exchange rate mechanism.

As an illustration, take the relatively simple case of Venezuela. There is a normal exchange rate (3.32–3.35 bolivares
per dollar) which applies to all transactions, except that there
are lower buying rates (3.05–3.09) for foreign exchange obtained from petroleum exports; this is equivalent to an export
tax and is the chief source of revenue for the government. The
only other exceptions relate to exchange received from exports
of coffee and cocoa, for which the Venezuela authorities pay
much higher than the normal rates (4.25–4.80) to encourage
diversification in the country. These last rates are somewhat
variable in their operation. When the world prices of these
products rise, part of the exchange proceeds are acquired at
normal rates on a basis which will provide the producers with
a stable average price in domestic currency. Venezuela, having
adequate reserves in dollars, does not use the multiple-rate

system as a control factor with reference to the balance of payments.

Other countries have much more complicated systems with the rates varying much more widely and frequently, and sometimes subdivided into many more categories. On the purchase of foreign exchange side, differentials may be used to encourage preferred exports; for example, to encourage the initial processing of raw materials before export, or to encourage tourism or investment. On the selling of foreign exchange side, the rates are frequently related roughly to such categories as essentials, less-essentials, luxuries, and financial transactions, frequently with an overtone of protection in the specific application. It may also be used to eliminate windfall profits from importing where the exchange rate does not correspond to the differences between prices in the two trading countries and there is a limit on the quantities which can be imported.

The use of multiple rates as a technique for balance-of-payments adjustments cannot be isolated from its use for the purposes described above. As an alternative to quantitative restrictions as a means of meeting balance-of-payments pressure, multiple exchange rates can be used to encourage as well as to discourage, to increase the amount of the country's resources devoted to exports and capital imports, or to reduce imports and capital exports. Such a system can function as though a devaluation had taken place for a part of a country's foreign transactions.

It should be noted that a multiple-rate system has been introduced in recent years in at least half a dozen countries with a free market outlet. In these instances, either a fixed part of foreign exchange receipts may be disposed of in a free market, or certain classes of transactions are handled in the free market, or the fixed-rate system is so operated as to be more favorable than the free market and thus it controls certain parts of the foreign trade but leaves the marginal transactions to be governed by the free market.

Multiple-rate systems can best be defended when the full burden of influencing the trade pattern is placed upon them and there is freedom for anybody to buy and sell according to the rate system. Since there are administrative limitations to the ability to control all transactions, particularly invisible and capital transactions, the effort to control needs to be concentrated on the trade items aimed at encouraging certain imports and exports. There then would be a higher rate for nonessential imports, but it must not be so high as to reward evasion and smuggling. The desired differential can be obtained if all transactions outside the essential area are permitted to be done in a free market, whose relationship to the fixed rates can be determined by shifts in the definition of essentiality.

The problems of multiple exchange rates are essentially those of any form of controls. In some circumstances, they may be preferable to quantitative restrictions which are more likely to lead to windfall profits and monopoly positions for licensed importers, and graft and corruption among the licensing officials. Clearly, the device is one which may be useful in the short run, but it must not be regarded as a satisfactory substitute for measures to correct a fundamental disequilibrium of the trade and payments situation—measures such as the use of appropriate fiscal and monetary policies and the general readjustment of exchange rates after a period of inflation. It raises the general problems related to specific controls discussed in Chapter II.

On the imports side, the choice in some cases might be regarded as lying between the use of multiple rates and tariffs. It is worth noting that tariffs are more permanent, usually related to treaties and parliamentary action, and that receipts in one case go to the treasury and in the other usually to the central bank. Since it is desirable to avoid increased restrictions in anything resembling a permanent form, there is at least an argument for the use of multiple rates, although this may expose the authorities to all the pressures usually associated with protectionist ambitions.

When multiple rates apply to exports, a different type of problem arises in the importing country. In the case of the United States, the law requires the Treasury to impose countervailing duties when imports are subject to subsidy. But if one commodity has a more favorable exchange rate than another (for example, the exporter of it receives double the amount of local currency for a given amount of dollars earned by export than the exporter of a different commodity), is a subsidy involved? Quite as logically, the fact that the other commodity receives less may be regarded as a tax. Whether one is subsidized or the other is taxed is really a matter of motivation. Certainly, if one viewed the situation in terms of the intent, few cases would appear where one could find a subsidy intended to lower prices abroad, although frequently it is intended to adjust to world prices. In most cases in Latin America, the tax interpretation is the more appropriate, although there are cases of infant industries for the foreign market, and here some form of export subsidy is more likely to exist. In fact, one of the basic objections to multiple rates lies in the fact that they can be used to move high cost exports and thus prevent the most efficient use of resources, both within the country and among countries.

All in all, in a world of various undesirably restrictive devices, the multiple exchange rate system has taken its place among the instruments of policy. Like all medicine, it should be taken with care, only when appropriate, and always with an eye towards getting along without it.

Cross–Rates

Payments may be made directly between two currencies or they may be made through a third currency or even more—dollars into Swiss francs into French francs, for example. Therefore, an established pattern of exchange rates involves not merely one country's bilateral rates, but rates between other countries. A country's trade and payments pattern may be affected by an exchange rate between two other countries. If the franc-dollar rate is changed and the franc-pound rate is not, this will affect the degree of direct interchange between sterling and dollars unless the dollar-pound rate is altered accordingly or unless controls are imposed.

The problem of cross-rates arises only when currencies are not convertible, for when they are, foreign exchange arbitrage will keep all channels in balance. Under such a free situation, if a large supply of a particular currency accumulates in one country and there is a relatively small supply in another, those in the second country will buy the desired currency in the first. The arbitrage mechanism breaks down when currencies are not convertible and transferable; then the two markets with their relative surplus and shortage will each require special action to restrict payments or trade to maintain the exchange rates. The inevitable result of the effort to maintain all rates in some fixed ratio to each other (to avoid breaking the cross-rates) is to take government action to support the weakening rate. This may involve the use of quantitative restrictions of one sort or another to achieve bilateral balance or the development of special currency or credit arrangements.

One interesting result of broken cross-rates is "commodity arbitrage" which might be called "exchange arbitrage by way of commodities." The prohibition of exchange arbitrage through transfers of balances (inconvertibility) still leaves open opportunities for exchange arbitrage through transshipment of goods. If the pound sterling falls relative to the dollar in the exchange market of a country that has heavily exported to Britain, business firms in the first country may use their otherwise unusable balances to buy goods from Britain and afterwards reship or switch them to a dollar country. Britain, of course, loses dollar exports through this switch.

Since restrictions already are altering the flow of commodities, it is difficult to determine whether these transactions improve the distribution of goods or not, though reactions to pressures usually tend to reduce the pressure. From the point of view of the authorities, such transactions circumvent the elaborate control and restrictive systems which have been set up in various countries. Also, commodity arbitrage is disliked by the established traders who suffer from the competition of importers who engage in such arrangements primarily as exchange operators rather than as commodity dealers.

Commodity shunting, although stimulated and facilitated by the existence of broken cross-rates, may take place even without broken cross-rates. Such switches may become profitable whenever exchange restrictions give the owner of a scarce currency a windfall profit that is not allowed to be reflected in the exchange rates. Certain control authorities, for example, permit dollar earners to keep part of the dollar proceeds of their exports for more liberal uses. Businessmen may then import from a soft-currency country and re-export to a dollar country in order to get hold of dollars, so valuable to them. The soft-currency country may have lost an opportunity for direct exports against dollars, depending upon whether it would have been profitable at the official rate or not.

Broken cross-rates are unpopular with most monetary authorities. They do not like to see the currency whose stability they are supposed to maintain decline in value in, or via any of, the foreign markets. Therefore, if exchange stability is their goal, broken cross-rates represent an undermining of their efforts at a point outside their control. The real question here is one of cause and effect. The broken cross-rate is a reflection of pressures and probably not a cause of them.

Basically, the measures which must be taken involve either some special commodity or exchange deals, the willingness to accumulate foreign exchange balances (a sort of compulsory loan), or trade restrictions. The problem of broken cross-rates therefore appears as a phenomenon related to systems of control, particularly where fixed exchange rates are maintained. Much depends upon the degree to which the efforts of the authorities are undermined, but the alternative is to use quantitative restrictions to balance bilateral trade between the debtor and creditor countries, involving differing degrees of discrimination. Broken cross-rates may be regarded as a step towards more realistic exchange rates and multilateral settlements.

FLUCTUATING RATES

In spite of the general approach established at Bretton Woods in favor of fixed exchange rates discussed at the beginning of this chapter, there have been various cases where fluctuating or floating exchange rates have been adopted and there is a considerable body of opinion which would support the further extension of the development. While there is a clear difference in concept between fixed and fluctuating rates, the distinction is not always so clear in practice. If a fixed rate is frequently revalued or a fluctuating rate is pegged within certain limits by government action, each loses some of its contrast with the other. Very few currency authorities who have adopted so-called fluctuating rates have in practice left the rate to emerge wholly from the action of market forces. It is the far more common practice for countries with fluctuating rates to support the rate for a considerable period and then to let the rate move upwards or downwards and renew support within some different limits. In practice, fluctuating rates regularly supported in this way by an exchange equalization fund may differ from fixed rates only in that the par value is not announced, that it swings within somewhat wider limits, and that no formality attaches to a change of rate. Under a fixed rate, the government is obligated to take supporting action when necessary; under a fluctuating rate what action it takes or fails to take is a matter of its discretion.

As a matter of fact, if the country is in reasonably satisfactory equilibrium, it probably does not matter greatly whether its exchange rate is fixed or fluctuating. Therefore, the real question is the relationship of the character of the rate to the process of correcting a disequilibrium. Here it must be clearly recognized that it is the level of the rate which is the force involved and therefore the problem comes back to the question of the wisdom of governments as against the market. For a world that is still in disequilibrium there is much to be said for an arrangement which would allow individual currencies to find their own levels. For it is arguable that one of the

major postwar errors was a too precipitate attempt to establish
the first set of par values. In several cases, e. g., Mexico in 1948–
49, the argument for permitting a fluctuating rate was to allow
it to " find its level," after which presumably it was to be
fixed again.

What is not yet clear is whether the concept enshrined in
the Bretton Woods agreement, the concept of a system of fixed
exchange rates subject to revision whenever substantially
changed circumstances require it, really provides a workable
system. It is clear that there is far greater reluctance for a
government to change a fixed rate than some of the sponsors
had hoped and that national pride not infrequently leads to a
too prolonged defense of an overvalued rate. Furthermore, the
consultative machinery for considering and approving changes
of rate has shown itself to be virtually unworkable in practice;
once a major country is determined to change a rate there is
little that the staff of the International Monetary Fund or the
Executive Directors can possibly do in the time available to
modify, or even to scrutinize fully, its proposals, and acceptance
can be little more than a formality.

Thus the attempts hitherto to work this system have not
led to the quick adjustment either of overvalued or of undervalued currencies, and it is arguable that some part of the difficulties of recent years has arisen from excessive anxiety to
defend fixed rates with the aid of the wide variety of exchange
controls and trade controls, both discriminatory and nondiscriminatory, with which governments have equipped themselves
during the past two decades.

Which method is most likely to encourage adjustments? In
the one case, the most apparent consequence of disequilibrium
is a falling exchange rate; in the other, the loss of reserves.
It is argued that, in a world in which money wages and other
money costs are difficult to reduce, it is substantially less likely
that a country will be driven to use severely deflationary measures if a balance can seemingly be restored through a shift in
the exchange rate. The pressure on a government to take the
necessary minimum of disinflationary action may be insufficient

if falling exchange rates automatically offset rising prices, whereas it would be obliged to take action to defend a fixed rate. Others argue that the very fact that a fluctuating rate is showing signs of falling will stimulate the government concerned to intervene.

The balance of probability is hard to judge from *a priori* argument, although it would seem reasonable to say that since the fluctuating rate is itself something of a corrective factor, governments will be required to a greater extent to take steps in other ways if the rate is fixed. The question is whether the action taken will be in the underlying monetary, fiscal, and structural areas, or will perhaps merely be to apply quantitative trade restrictions more severely.

Just how helpful fluctuating rates would be as guides to economic action raises the basic question of the relative wisdom of governments and markets. Fluctuating rates correspond to price activity in a market economy. The arguments in support of fixed rates have already been presented, but it must also be noted that a fluctuating rate would be subject to all forces directed to the market arising from both trade and capital movements. These two factors do not necessarily act in parallel, and the desired effect on either one might be offset by factors influencing the other. How important this may be depends upon the extent to which the authorities may have some other economic plan in mind. Freely fluctuating prices seek to establish an equilibrium, but that may not correspond to the allocation of resources required by other national objectives.

In the case of non-key currencies, there might now be some advantages in a system which would permit the rate to fluctuate. This has been apparent both from Canadian experience in using such a rate and from the experience of some countries where the multiple-rate system has sometimes provided, in effect, the equivalent of a fluctuating rate on an important marginal component of total trade.

It is more debatable whether it is desirable to have fluctuating relations between the major currencies of the world in which a large part of the trade is conducted. A fluctuating rate by definition is fluctuating in relation to some more fixed element. It is perhaps possible to relate all the fluctuations to the gold price. But in effect what countries are concerned about is their relation to the dollar or to sterling or both. It would provide a much firmer anchor for the fluctuations of minor currencies if the dollar and the pound, plus possibly one or two other key currencies, could be assumed to bear a fixed relation. There is, moreover, a rather special aspect of the virtues of fixity where a currency is used as a central banking and reserve standard by a large number of other countries.

On the other hand, occasionally heavy revaluations of a fixed rate may be more disturbing to the countries using these key currencies than a nominally fluctuating rate which is supported in practice for long periods of time at more or less recognized points. The relationship of the pound and the dollar fluctuated without very grave inconvenience for a considerable period in the 1930's, and exchange futures markets were sufficiently active to make it possible for the ordinary trader to hedge against short-term fluctuations at comparatively low cost.

There is no agreement that any far-reaching overhaul of the system created at Bretton Woods is called for, so far as it concerns exchange rates. The system as a whole has not yet been put into full operation and is virtually untried in many of its aspects. Until the world achieves a genuine postwar balance, it is too early to say that the exchange provisions and objectives were misguided. What can, however, be said is that, if the world is to move toward the reduction of restrictions designed simply to defend overvalued currencies, there may be need to reconsider the relative values of some currencies, and to perfect the arrangements for doing this.

Under the present provisions of its Articles, the International Monetary Fund is virtually powerless to take the initiative in encouraging the gradual removal of restrictions through mutual reciprocal negotiation. The gradual and mutual removal of controls and the readjustment of exchange rates require continuous and multilateral negotiation. This is not easy to achieve. The success of EPU may be due to the degree of common approach by a regional group, while the world-wide character of the Fund and the permanence of the Executive Board, whose members are therefore separated from policy-making functions at home, may make it an unsatisfactory forum for such negotiations. But, at least, with its staff and its prestige and in view of the persistence of the " transition " period, perhaps it should be encouraged to take a more active role.

BLACK MARKETS

The systems described above do not define the extent of flexibility in exchange transactions today. Commodity shunting transactions, mentioned in connection with the exploitation of broken cross-rates, are only one form of a very large variety of ways of getting around some of the existing foreign exchange controls. There are many methods in the financial field for arranging payments outside of official channels. In these transactions, rates are frequently different from those in regular channels, and currencies are converted and payments made which would otherwise be restricted. Since most of these transactions violate the laws of one or more countries in spirit if not in letter, they are called " black market " dealings.

Black markets are reported to transfer substantial amounts of foreign exchange. It was estimated, though obviously the facts are not matters of record, that in New York alone the turnover in various kinds of pound sterling in May, 1953, averaged $1 million a day. This includes transactions which are not strictly illegal but nevertheless are beyond the scope of normal commercial bank operations.

The greater part of black market transactions in foreign exchange is connected with blocked accounts, with legal and illegal gold movements, and with the large-scale smuggling of diamonds. Involved in many of the black market dealings in foreign exchange is the forgery or " irregular " issuance of official certificates such as custom receipts or certificates of origin or destination, although only a few of the parties to such transactions may be aware of it.

The moral climate and social discipline of countries is sufficiently different to explain why in certain countries the black marketeer is not always held in the same contempt as other law breakers. Where governments enact and enforce their foreign exchange regulations efficiently, honestly, and with a minimum of personal discrimination, as part of an economic policy generally accepted as reasonable and realistic, the community is more likely to accept the regulations and support their enforcement. But this may not be sufficient to avoid substantial evasion and circumvention of the exchange regulations. Even the economics of control can rely more safely on operations reflecting price and profit incentives than on automatic conformance with governmental restrictions and prohibitions. However, at this point, it is sufficient to recognize that there is more exchange flexibility and convertibility in practice than appears on the record.

CHAPTER VII

Problems of Convertibility

AN important function of money is to facilitate indirect exchange. By being generally acceptable as a medium of exchange, money enables people to sell in one market and buy in another. While money readily fulfills this function within the borders of most countries except on occasions of extreme inflation, governments from time to time have imposed restrictions on the foreign use of money, limiting its convertibility into foreign currencies and even making it difficult or unlawful for a seller to use the money received from his sales in one country to purchase from that same or from another country.

During the nineteenth and early twentieth centuries, the use of currencies in international transactions was seldom subject to interference by governments. The institution of the gold standard, with its convertibility of local currency into gold, assured relative stability of exchange rates between different currencies and thus further facilitated triangular and multilateral trade. The absence of restrictions on the interchangeability of currencies and the presence of institutions to provide such interchanges promoted multilateral trade in increasing volume and encouraged substantial international flows of capital. Neither an exporter of goods nor an exporter of capital had to worry about getting caught with nontransferable balances abroad or about getting rid of foreign exchange only with severe losses. Neither an importer of goods nor a debtor trying to repay had to worry about not being able to obtain the foreign currency needed for his payments. International settlements were on a multilateral basis. Convertibility existed because nationals were allowed to trade freely in all foreign currencies without interference. However, it does not require a private market and convertibility would also exist if a government stood ready to buy and sell foreign currencies without limit.

THE LIMITS OF CONVERTIBILITY

It has already been made abundantly clear that the nineteenth century does not provide a picture of the economic world today. Nearly all countries have limitations upon the degree to which their currencies may be converted into other currencies. But the trade of each country is by nature in part triangular, that is, there is an inevitable tendency for a surplus to arise in trade with some countries and a deficit to arise with others. The advantages of multilateral trade need no elaboration at this point, in its relation both to the use of resources and to the level of trade itself. Absence of convertibility implies that the surpluses cannot be utilized for the financing of the deficits. Since one country's bilateral deficit is another's surplus, the blocking of a balance somewhere along the line tends to affect settlement within the whole circuit of multilateral payment. Accordingly, instead of having to deal with national payment disequilibria which can be overcome one at a time, this situation presents one indivisible international disequilibrium which is not readily subject to national solution. In another respect, inconvertibility restrains trade. If surpluses are inconvertible, countries cannot afford to accumulate them (they really are a form of credit extension) and will find the means of preventing or limiting their growth.

The change in the payments position of the United Kingdom is important in its effect upon multilateral settlement, for it has greatly affected the position of Continental Europe which can no longer count on the United Kingdom as the country ready to absorb export surpluses and thus supply currency for financing imports from other continents. In a sense, what the United Kingdom lost, its former debtor countries have gained, and had they been willing or able to purchase European manufactured goods in increased quantities, the situation would not be so serious. But the old triangles have been slow in reasserting themselves, and new ones have had little chance to develop.

Certain trade patterns have grown up within the framework of trade and currency controls directed at bilateral balance. Convertibility would inevitably change these patterns, and therefore raise many of the problems that are associated with any lowering of trade barriers. However, the benefits to exporters seem clearer than the threat to importers (which is not specific) and removing restrictions on the use of currency has never developed the same heat as has similar action in the tariff field.

Given the great desirability of multilateral trade, what are the limits to which convertibility can be extended, the conditions under which earnings in one currency can be convertible into another, and the extent to which preference should be given to certain groups of applicants for foreign exchange or to certain purposes, if all cannot be accommodated?

The extent to which the authorities responsible for any currency can permit its conversion into another currency depends ultimately on their power to acquire the demanded currency and on the scale of demands for it which will be presented to them. If all demands can be met, there is no problem. If only a fraction of demands can be met, there is need for some procedure of rationing and ultimately of correcting the basic difficulty, whatever it may be.

The volume of demand to convert from one currency into another will obviously depend on the relative attractiveness of the two currencies for purchases of goods or services and for holding as reserve. That is to say, convertibility will present a problem to a country if a currency is overvalued or if the structure of an economy and its trade problem are still in process of adjustment to the ruling exchange rate. It will present no immediate problem if the currency is undervalued or if the structures of the economy and of the outside world are still in process of adjustment after a period of undervaluation.

At the present time, except in a very small number of countries, foreign currencies are either bought and sold by governments or are controlled by the issuance of licenses. Within any given total of earnings of the second currency, the authorities controlling the first currency can only increase its convertibility for some purposes by diminishing its convertibility for other purposes. They may, if they wish, make the currency more convertible by foreign holders while making it less convertible by domestic holders. They may make it more freely convertible by all holders by creating conditions in which the demands of all holders for conversion are diminished by increasing the obstacles to trade such as quantitative restrictions. They can only make the currency more convertible by everyone, within a given level of restrictions to trade, if they can increase the total of the second currency available. It is possible that the removal of restrictions and the fact of convertibility itself may contribute to enlarging the earnings in the second currency or to reducing the demand for it. But it is unlikely, unless equilibrium is nearer than the currency authorities have supposed, that the whole adjustment can come from this source.

Convertibility and Discrimination

Since various currencies may have differing degrees of hardness, an individual country experiencing difficulty in balancing its surpluses and its deficits cannot easily obtain relief through the use of nondiscriminatory policies such as exchange depreciation or deflation. These affect its whole situation vis-a-vis the rest of the world and only fortuitously its various bilateral balances. Rather it is necessary to discriminate among countries according to whether their currency is harder or softer, and the result is likely to be to divert trade into second-best channels involving less efficient producers, higher prices, and reduced advantage from trade.

If full convertibility is regarded as immediately impracticable, for what purposes and to what groups should preference be given?

It is possible to group the holders of the currency whose conversion into some other currency may be asked, into certain broad categories among which some degree of administrative discrimination is practicable (additional subclassifications are possible) :

(1) All residents of the currency-issuing country;

(2) All residents of countries which employ for international currency purposes the same currency or one very closely associated with it (e. g., sterling area countries in relation to sterling) ;

(3) Non-residents who are residents in the country of issue of the desired currency (e. g., Americans wanting to change sterling into dollars) ;

(4) All non-residents other than those included in (2) or (3) ;

(5) Central banks of countries included in (2) ;

(6) All other central banks.

To illustrate these categories, sterling is at present freely convertible into dollars by holders in categories (3) and (5). The demand under (3) is limited by tariffs and quantitative restrictions. The demand under (5) is governed by the restrictions imposed by the sterling area countries individually, but usually after discussion with London. Sterling is not freely convertible into dollars by domestic holders of sterling either in the United Kingdom (1) or the sterling area (2). Dollars are the ordinary means of settlement with certain additional countries in the so-called " dollar " area, but the trade with other countries is normally conducted in sterling and certain conditions are attached to its transferability between holders.

The general practice of the sterling area and of most European countries is broadly analogous to that of the United Kingdom. Convertibility into gold or dollars is rather widely confined to other central banks' holdings under certain agreed conditions, to certain agreed fractions of holdings acquired by the European Payments Union, and to holdings by residents in the dollar currency countries and certain other countries which have been included in the dollar area.

It is possible to discriminate also among the types of transactions which have led to the holdings whose conversion will or will not be approved. Conversion may be permitted of holdings in the local currency acquired from the sale of imports approved in each individual case by license or permit; it may be permitted for all imports covered by a general license for a particular category; it may be permitted for certain types of proposed capital movements arising from certain transactions but not from others; it may be permitted, in the limiting case, for all transactions, both current and capital, with no questions asked. In practice, convertibility in a good many cases is an automatic consequence of the approval of an import license or of the extension of a general license.

It is also possible to discriminate according to the use to be made of the scarce currency which is being rationed. Thus, treatment may be different for those who wish to purchase goods for import, purchase goods abroad for sale in third countries, travel abroad, buy foreign securities, obtain foreign currency, or build up deposits abroad.

The regulations governing convertibility may vary according to the foreign currency involved. For many countries, there are some currencies which are harder than their own (harder might be defined as harder to get) and others which are softer. Obviously, the treatment of the two groups may vary considerably. Full convertibility would occur when any holder, regardless of how he came into possession of a currency and regardless of how he plans to use the foreign currency, may convert into the foreign currency without interference. Complete inconvertibility would occur when no one would be able to utilize his balances in a country for any kind of foreign transaction. So long as some currencies are hard, like dollars, in the sense that sums of dollars available from trade, aid, or American foreign investment are below the sum of all the demands for dollars at the prevailing exchange rates, different exchange controls have rung the changes as best they could on the threefold basis of possible choice among applicants, source, and use. The three types of limitation are related in the sense that, since the purpose is to cut the transactions eligible for conversion to the amount of foreign currency available, restriction of any one type reduces the necessity for restricting according to the others.

It is possible, within a given limit of scarce currency earnings, to make the operation of exchange controls liberal by imposing such restrictions on trade that the demand for the scarce currency is greatly reduced. In the limiting case, the exchange control could be wholly removed by transferring all its functions to trade controls. There is very general agreement that such a change would not really improve matters, that convertibility and liberalization are joint objectives and not alternatives. There would be little point in achieving convertibility in the financial sense, if progress towards trade liberalization had to be reversed to obtain it.

As a matter of fact, there is a real likelihood that under certain circumstances an extension of convertibility will lead to increased discrimination. For example, a country which undertakes to convert into dollars any of its currency earned by nonresidents on current account, would be under strong compulsions to continue a system of bilateral trade arrangements with other soft currency countries. By this method, it would be possible to achieve a mutual increase in trade above the level permitted by its general level of nondiscriminatory restrictions without creating an added threat to the reserves. Otherwise, trade must be held at levels calculated on the basis of possible settlement in gold or dollars.

In judging what is desirable and what are the probable implications and costs of alternative policies, it is relevant to bear in mind that some of the controls over the transferability of currencies between foreign holders are almost impossible to enforce and that there is a great deal of evasion, seldom in the interests of the types of trade that the program is intended to promote.

At the present time, a holder of dollars is able to convert them into other currencies almost anywhere in the world. There are two other systems of convertibility within geographical limits which deserve special mention, the sterling area and the European Payments Union.

THE STERLING AREA

The significance of the sterling area can best be appreciated in the light of its origin and development. Before the first World War, Britain was the chief middleman, shipper, insurer, and banker of the world; the gold standard was essentially a sterling standard and London held the working balances of many countries, as well as their external reserves. Most of the world's clearing was done on the books of the London banks. Even between the two wars the position of Britain as a financial and trading center was still important enough to make a large group of countries decide to follow Britain in the devaluation of 1931 and to be part of the sterling bloc, although there was no particular uniformity in their behavior otherwise. A much smaller group combined to adhere to the sterling area within which exchange control did not operate, when it took legal shape under defense regulations just before the second World War. At present the sterling area includes Burma, Iraq, Ireland, and Iceland besides the United Kingdom, the Colonies, and the other Commonwealth countries (except Canada). (The Union of South Africa is a special kind of member, maintaining its own reserves but selling gold for sterling according to agreement.)

The essential features of the sterling area are (1) absence of restrictions on current payments among residents of the area, (2) general license for tourist traffic with unlimited use of funds within the area, (3) absence in most sterling area countries of restrictions on capital movements to other sterling area countries, (4) exercise of exchange control over dealings with non-residents of the sterling area, (5) exercise of import restrictions by a system of licensing imposed by each country independently, though in occasional consultation with other governments of the sterling area countries, (6) pooling of dollar reserves with an obligation to surrender dollar earnings (except from certain gold exports) to the central pool in exchange for sterling balances, and (7) the right of member governments to draw freely on this dollar pool against payment in sterling, although this latter right is limited to a degree in practice as may be required to protect the reserves.

The sterling area was probably in dollar surplus before the war, but remained in heavy current dollar deficit in the immediate postwar years, making its payments from assets, borrowing, and aid. A large part of the decline in the gold and dollar reserves of the sterling pool may be attributed to the deficits of the countries of the outer sterling area, although these were not all dollar deficits. The three largest countries in the outer area, Australia, South Africa, and India, had a total postwar net deficit on current account of almost $4 billions. This was financed partly by drawing on their sterling balances and partly by movements of private capital from the United Kingdom. On the other hand, in the five years 1948–52, the United Kingdom had surpluses on current account in every year except 1951, the net surplus for the period totaling over $700 millions.

During the postwar period, there have been three " crisis " periods when the dollar reserves of the sterling area have been drawn down so rapidly as to require drastic action. In 1947, an attempt at convertibility led to such rapid exchange of sterling for dollars that the experiment had to be stopped in a few weeks. In 1949, a loss of reserves was met first by increased restrictions on dollar trade and then by devaluation. In 1951, a similar loss of reserves was met by trade restrictions. One result of this changing state of affairs has been that trade within the area has been more stable than with the rest of the world.

The operation of the sterling area provides convertibility so far as trade within the area is concerned, a system of settlements among the members, and a more or less consolidated balance-of-payments position towards the rest of the world. The system permits a member like the United Kingdom, which may be in surplus within the area but in dollar deficit, to acquire dollars that have been earned by other members. On the other hand, the dollars made available to the United Kingdom through United States aid, particularly the Anglo-American loan, became part of the sterling area resources and became accessible to other members to meet their needs in covering their current balances in non-sterling countries. Before the war, if there was a drain on a country's reserves, it had to take action. Now it has recourse to the common reserve through the sterling balances and the whole system is affected because of the thin margin.

The fact that the system is made up of a significantly wide variety of economies probably provides a greater stability in exchange rates for the member countries than would be possible if each country operated independently. Nevertheless, this inevitably creates certain strains within the area. The first is between the dollar surplus and dollar deficit countries. If a country is in the first group, it may well feel that there is little advantage in membership since part of its dollar earnings must go to support the requirements of the other members. In fact, any member purchasing in sterling from another member uses up some of its balance and therefore some of its rights to draw on the dollar pool, so that there is probably less incentive for intra-sterling pool trade than is usually assumed. Countries in surplus may relax import controls or even seek to build up their own gold reserves, for most of the time each country imposes its trade restrictions independently in accordance with its own needs. (Countries in the sterling area have the right to retain some gold without putting it in the central pool.)

The second strain appears in connection with the flow of capital. In the past, capital and capital goods for economic development were largely provided by the United Kingdom. This still has been substantial in the postwar period partly through so-called unrequited exports (liquidation of sterling balances accumulated during the war). For the underdeveloped countries, access to the capital market was an important factor in their interest in sterling. How much London can re-establish itself as a capital market is therefore an important consideration with respect to the future of the sterling area.

The third strain has to do with handling crisis situations.

Under the circumstances, a crisis for the sterling area may arise from some general cause or from the unwise actions of some of the member countries. There is no secretariat and no standing arrangement for consultation. The Bank of England keeps in contact with the other monetary authorities, there is exchange of information through the Sterling Area Statistical Committee, and from time to time finance ministers may be assembled. There is no doubt but that the informality of the arrangements permits misunderstandings and prevents quick formulation and endorsement of common policy. In fact, if one can generalize from two cases, it might be said that the machinery is able to check a run on reserves only after a loss of about $2 billions.

Much of the significance as well as the difficulties of the sterling area arrangements would disappear if conditions permitted more general convertibility to be achieved. In the meantime, it does provide a substantial area of trade and economic activity within which exchange difficulties are limited. On the other hand, it is widely believed that in the long run, the pound sterling cannot maintain its position as a major international currency unless other countries are willing to hold working balances in sterling. This they are most likely to do if sterling becomes convertible, since the decline in importance of the United Kingdom as a capital exporter and as an international commodity market reduces the scope for the use of sterling. The prewar system was built on the acceptability of sterling and this in turn rested on the expectation that sterling would be as hard as any other currency.

European Payments Union (EPU)

A second institution has brought a substantial degree of convertibility into this troubled economic world. As described in Chapter V, the European Payments Union (EPU) is a creation and part of the Organization for European Economic Cooperation (OEEC). Its chief contribution is a clearing mechanism with provisions for credit extension among the

member countries. Its actual operations are handled by the
Bank for International Settlements (BIS) in Basel.

The EPU comprises sixteen countries of Europe and
through its members also settles the European accounts of
various overseas areas in close monetary relations with European countries such as the members of the sterling area, the
franc area, and the overseas territories of Belgium, Portugal,
the Netherlands, and Indonesia. These countries and areas
carry on among themselves something like two-fifths of the
world's international trade and another fifth with other countries, largely those of North and South America.

The compensation mechanism of the EPU does not deal
with individual transactions among residents of the countries or
areas concerned, but only the monthly net external positions
not cleared within the banking systems of the countries involved. These net positions added up to $20 billions in the
period between July, 1950, and June, 1953. Of this amount
$15 billions or 75 per cent was liquidated by multilateral off-
setting within the Union, 8 per cent was settled by gold payments, 10 per cent by EPU credits, and the remainder by
various " pre-quota operations " connected largely with debt
payments and residual United States aid.

The extension of credits to countries running a debit balance with the EPU is made possible in part through a dollar
reserve provided by the United States, but mostly through
credits which countries running a credit balance automatically
grant by their accumulation of such credit balances. The
obligations to grant these credits to the EPU as well as the
rights to be in debt with the EPU are limited by agreed quotas
with stipulated percentages to be settled in gold. A country
in surplus does not receive payment until its accumulated
credit balance reaches 20 per cent of its quota; thereafter it can
demand 50 per cent of its monthly credit balance in gold but
has to leave the rest with the EPU up to the agreed quota. (A
country does not yet receive 100 per cent even after its quota
is exceeded.) A country in deficit has to make no payment
until its accumulated debit balance reaches 20 per cent of its

quota. It must pay gold for 20 per cent of its monthly deficit if its accumulated debit balance is between 20 and 40 per cent of its quota. The ratio of gold payment to credit continues thus to rise until it has to pay 100 per cent of its monthly deficit in gold when its quota has been exhausted.

At the same time that these progressive rates tend to discourage excessive deficits, they have had less influence in affecting the policies of creditors. Actually, influence is exerted in another way, for the situation is kept under continuous observation by a managing group with limited, but in fact fairly extensive, powers. This provides a framework for constant review, discussion, and negotiation.

The managing group and the OEEC have concerned themselves increasingly with the problems and policies of individual countries. Although there have been large swings in the position of most countries over time, some countries have become extreme debtors or extreme creditors and remained in that position for a considerable period. While the creditors have so far agreed to grant additional credits beyond their quotas, the debtors have been under the full discipline of the requirement for 100 per cent gold or dollar payments. Too often, however, they have tended to fall back upon trade restrictions again, thus undercutting the mutuality of the liberalization scheme. It is to encourage other forms of action which will check stubborn debtor or creditor positions that the consultations are held.

Nevertheless, there is real hesitancy in considering as a group one type of action the possible need of correcting inappropriate exchange rate patterns. The fixed exchange rates of a country may be seriously out of line, chiefly because domestic fiscal and monetary policies may have engendered inflationary pressures on incomes and prices. Such a country, adhering to its adopted exchange rate, will soon exhaust its borrowing rights and, facing a loss of gold commensurate to its imports, will reimpose all the quantitative import restrictions that it may have given up under the EPU rules. But if EPU were to concern itself with such a situation, it might lead to a real jurisdictional question with the IMF. Furthermore, this is one area in which all national officials are exceedingly uncommunicative and sensitive. However, the point of greatest substance here is that a change in exchange rate cannot be applied regionally and must necessarily be judged in terms of its over-all impact. It cannot be focussed on a regional disequilibrium.

The built-in trade liberalization scheme already discussed is one of the most useful parts of the EPU–OEEC system. As a member of OEEC, each country (the obligation does not extend to the overseas territories) is expected to free stipulated fractions of its total imports from quantitative restrictions unless its balance-of-payments situation with the rest of the area is too unfavorable, which its position within EPU would indicate. Thus, a semi-automatic scheme of removing direct import controls supplements the incentive-effects which the multilateral settlement system has with regard to nondiscriminatory import restrictions. Each country can be indifferent as to which of the other member countries becomes its best customer or its best supplier because all surpluses are settled partly in gold and dollars and partly in credit balances which are automatically convertible into any of the currencies involved. Hence, there is no advantage in discriminating among different importers or exporters, and the principle of buying in the cheapest markets and selling where the price is highest (within the region) can again be followed.

One of the defects of the system stems directly from its regional character, that the lending obligations and borrowing rights are determined on the basis of regional rather than global balance-of-payments patterns. A poor country, like Italy or Portugal, might be forced into piling up EPU balances and thus in effect exporting capital to richer countries like Sweden and Switzerland, when the former happens to incur its deficits outside Europe and the latter inside.

A third problem is the relationship of the region to external disturbances. There are those who feel that there is a great advantage in a common regional front. On the other hand, when the sterling area's difficulties in 1951 necessitated substantial back-tracking on trade liberalization, the impact was felt through all the EPU countries. However, it is likely that this would have happened, EPU or no EPU. The main point is that, while a region can be strengthened, it does not cover its members' extra-regional economic relationships and cannot therefore provide the whole solution.

Various possibilities suggest themselves for strengthening the operation of the EPU. Tighter rules seem called for in connection with the suspension and re-establishment of trade liberalization. Consideration should be given to extending the trade liberalization idea to overseas territories and possibly even to a coordinated effort to liberalize toward the dollar area. Some scheme needs to be devised for amortizing past credit positions and providing additional resources for credit extension.

While some critics have been inclined to see in the EPU machinery a " gadget " encouraging member countries to delay the restoration of full convertibility of their currencies and others have viewed it as dangerous encouragement of regional autarchy (note the Belgian case, Chapter V), it is now fairly generally agreed that membership in EPU has been of great assistance in establishing multilateral and freer trade at least on a regional basis. The limitations of the organization and operation must not be overlooked, but the system is, at least for a substantial part of the world, an approximation to full convertibility and has achieved substantial reductions in quantitative restrictions without which convertibility has only limited meaning.

RESERVE REQUIREMENTS

The possibility of increasing the area of convertibility is related to the problem of reserves. The function of exchange reserves is to allow a country to take the shock of an unexpected movement in its balance of payments. Such a shock may either be felt by a single country as a result of some isolated calamity in its own economy, or by a large number of countries simultaneously, due to a widespread recession in business activity or an extensive fall (or rise) in prices. Under present conditions, reserves alone cannot overcome a continuing disequilibrium since a flow of reserves is no longer intimately related to credit and currency behavior, but their use does provide time in which other methods of dealing with the situation can be brought into operation.

It might be argued that reserves are never too large. But since at present most countries have inadequate reserves by almost any standard and since the building up and maintaining of reserves involve substantial social cost, it is important to consider what minimum reserves are necessary. Here again, the reserves required are of course related to the volume of trade and the degree of freedom in the international economy, particularly the extent of convertibility.

Among the important factors affecting reserve requirements are: (a) the force of the shocks anticipated, (b) the probable source of such shocks, (c) the size of external liabilities and the probable response of creditors when a deficit appears (e. g., capital flight), (d) range of supplementary reserves (e. g., stocks of commodities), (e) accessibility to alternative means of settlement (e. g., foreign investments, credits), (f) effectiveness of and length of time required for actions to check a drain on reserves (e. g., higher rates of interest, quantitative restrictions, devaluation).

It follows that it is practically impossible to calculate some one figure as the optimum level of reserves for any given country. Nevertheless, individuals involved in international transactions are certain to form judgments as to whether reserves are clearly inadequate or clearly excessive, and their judgments will affect their behavior.

It is clear that the function of reserves today is quite different from the days when the shifting of reserves from one country to another was itself a major source of correction for the disequilibrium. There were active speculators in exchange and short-term credit facilities which tended to stabilize situations of disturbance, particularly if they were such localized shocks as a crop failure. The IMF credit facilities were intended to serve this same function, but it has been loath to use up its lending power to a country before that country has reached equilibrium. The IMF has felt that its credit resources were to aid in the maintenance of balance, rather than in achieving it in the first place.

Many suggestions have been made to meet the present situation where many countries have very low reserves. One would be to increase the common pool in the IMF. Another would be some sort of international machinery which would provide for automatic lending by creditor countries but without corresponding automatic borrowing rights by debtor countries, thus permitting negotiation to take place looking towards correcting the debtor's position. (One might add that conceivably some adjustment might be needed in the creditor's policies, also.)

Probably the most important uncertainty here is the scale of the shock against which the reserve is required. This raises the question of the degree to which the world must prepare itself for short-term or cyclical swings. The recessions of 1937–38 and 1949, while relatively small in the United States as recessions go, created major disturbances in international economic relations. In the United Nations study, "Measures for International Economic Stability," the experts put the drain on the reserves of the rest of the world at $10 billions current dollars in the event of a slump like that of 1937–38.

Some United States imports are elastic, dropping rapidly with a slight decline in the level of industrial production. They are products whose prices are highly sensitive to fluctuations in demand. This trade is of much greater importance in the economic life of the exporting countries than it is to the United States, and their imports in turn are much more essential. The result is that even a slight recession in the United States is likely to put a severe strain on other economies and their reserves would decline rapidly. The most likely pattern would be a draft on reserves followed by increased quantitative restrictions and reduced convertibility. The very minimum of reserves would be an amount sufficient to carry on the existing level of trade not only until new restrictions had been established but until there was time for a lower level of imports to be reflected in the balance-of-payments situation.

Next Steps Toward Convertibility

There seems to be widespread agreement that a world monetary system is needed which would make the best possible provision for multilateral trade and payments. The economist's ideal of convertibility is represented by unlimited freedom to exchange currencies in a world in which the demand for currencies arising from trade and payments is itself unfettered by trade restrictions of any sort, and in which all resources are fully employed in the ways that yield the greatest comparative advantage. This is, of course, an ideal, and the question is, how fast and how far can further progress be made, if any?

It has been pointed out that convertibility has many limited forms, legal or effective, regional or global, formal or material. It may be established unilaterally or multilaterally; it may be one-way convertibility or two-way convertibility; it may constitute a promise by the monetary authorities or merely a permission to buy or sell; and it may be at fixed foreign exchange rates or at adjustable rates or at completely free rates. Usually, current proposals are to move *toward* full convertibility, but they fall considerably short of the ideal.

They are briefly discussed below in three different frames of reference—convertibility for sterling, convertibility through the further development of EPU, and convertibility on a broader basis, related to the IMF.

Much current discussion has turned about increasing the degree of convertibility of sterling into dollars. Various individuals have varied in the boldness of their proposals, but what has been officially discussed is not full convertibility in the sense of the removal of the trade and exchange controls around the sterling area but partial convertibility in the more limited sense of extending convertibility to all non-resident current account sterling. In practice, Canadian and American account sterling is already convertible, and theoretically this is also true of sterling held by central banks of the sterling area. The remaining sterling balances are held either by EPU countries or by " the rest of the world." It is only these last two which would be directly affected by the proposed extension of convertibility. Meanwhile, controls would be continued over all imports into the sterling area, limiting in practice the amount of sterling in the accounts which might seek to be converted. It may be assumed that in any case control over capital movements would continue.

Before considering this " next step," it is necessary to examine the present economic situation in this particular context. There has undoubtedly been a marked improvement everywhere since 1947. There has been a substantial rise in production and consumption and in the volume of world trade. Nevertheless, the present state of partial equilibrium is precarious for reasons such as the following:

(1) The United States economy is operating at a high level which is reflected both in income and imports. It is unlikely that this will continue indefinitely without some recession. Many believe that a decline in United States production is associated with a much bigger drop in imports, especially sterling area imports.

(2) The present availability of dollars is partly due to United States offshore purchases and other overseas military expenditure which cannot be assumed to continue. United States economic aid is still significant in amount, but is likely to be reduced or eliminated if signs of economic strength appear.

(3) Dollar purchases by the sterling area are still strictly controlled and quite possibly the present level of dollar imports still reflects the severe cuts imposed in 1952. An improvement in the position of the sterling area will almost certainly be followed by some increased dollar expenditure.

(4) The central reserves of the sterling area are increasing

but still low, so that even a slight change in the economic climate adverse to the sterling area can develop swiftly into a crisis.

(5) It is not to be expected that much more gold can be withdrawn from the EPU.

(6) In Britain and to some extent in the rest of the sterling area, there are still quite strong tendencies towards a wage-cost inflation, and it is not yet certain that these can be overcome under conditions of full employment.

Undoubtedly, these uncertainties explain why fuller convertibility is not being proposed. Some sort of compulsion has led to the partial convertibility suggestion, although it is fair to say that this was part of a package proposal. It would be difficult to argue against the widening of the convertibility area *per se*, although it may not mean all that the phrase implies. In a sense, the sterling area has a given amount of current dollar earnings which at the moment it divides between adding to reserves and selling to certain applicants who have dollar payments to make. The proposal would be to add certain applicants to the list of those who can freely buy dollars for sterling.

The United Kingdom proposal for partial convertibility seems likely to present a striking contrast between the freedom to be granted to the residents of third countries to convert sterling into dollars, and the restrictions which the United Kingdom and the sterling area would continue upon their own residents. Politically this might prove difficult to maintain. It might be hard to convince the British people that they must continue to go without food, nylons, and machinery so that others can import American cars.

Moreover, if, as must be assumed, non-resident holders will desire to convert sterling into dollars, they may be expected to aim at maximizing their sterling balances available for this purpose by cutting down purchases from the sterling area. At the same time, in order to prevent too large an outflow of dollars, the United Kingdom may feel obliged to take steps to check the accumulation of sterling in the hands of potential converters. This they would do by cutting down imports from the countries to which the convertibility privilege was being extended. The only alternative would be to restrict the dollar imports of the sterling area still further, so that dollars previously available to it could be diverted to meet the non-resident demand.

So long as the pound was inconvertible, trade with third countries with equally soft or softer currencies could be liberalized at a high level. But this level is possible because of discrimination. To maintain the level if convertibility were substituted for exchange control might require import taxes or quantitative restrictions as discriminatory in character as the pre-existing exchange control and restrictions. The net gain from convertibility might therefore depend upon how far the gains from increased freedom in the utilization of dollars exceeded the loss of European or sterling area liberalization. Because of the dominant nature of the dollar-sterling problem, there has been a tendency to overlook relationships with other currencies, but the broader problem must be dealt with if any program is to be successful.

Any move towards convertibility would involve an added strain on the reserves if, as is to be assumed, the existing controls hold back an unsatisfied demand. If convertibility were combined with limitations of the right to use quantitative restrictions, it might be necessary to fall back on deflation or devaluation. The former involves the possible loss of production and employment, the latter deterioration in the terms of trade. It is a matter of argument how serious this may be. If in fact it is merely lack of competitiveness in the sterling economy which causes the trouble, then quite a small adjustment might make British industry competitive and close the gap. But if the causes of the trouble are more structural, then the depreciation might have to be much more severe.

An attempt to achieve convertibility on anything more than the most limited scale seems then to be related to certain prerequisites:

(1) The existence of a dollar surplus for the sterling area

so as to allow for the effect of relaxing dollar import controls. It is of course possible that the sterling balances might be a source of embarrassment, though if they were convertible there might be an even greater willingness to leave them on deposit as sterling.

(2) Very much larger reserves. Some estimates have suggested that reserves of the order of seven to eight billion dollars are needed to work a system of full convertibility (in the absence of quantitative restrictions) without undue risks; others would put the figure much lower, having in mind that in recent years it has been possible for the sterling area twice to check a run on its reserves after a loss of about $2 billions. This would imply that the same restrictions would be used again, in which case convertibility loses its meaning.

(3) The further development of substitute sources in the sterling area and Europe for dollar goods. These, however, would have to be produced at costs which would eventually be reasonably competitive. There is reason to believe that purposive action by governments could lead to successful projects of this kind. It is less likely that progress will be made with them if there is a continual possibility of immediate convertibility.

(4) A not inconsiderable body of opinion in other countries would add the necessity for some kind of safeguard against the danger of recession in the United States. If such a recession begins, it is possible that the United Kingdom may wish to take the lead in forming a regional grouping to maintain a high level of trade among the members. The skeptics of convertibility would wish to be assured either that the possibility of a swift retreat into such a system was not debarred or that the United States was somehow committed to maintaining a sufficient flow of dollars.

In view of all the difficulties and uncertainties, it has been argued that any approach to sterling convertibility should be a gradual one. Progress is in fact being made. Sterling area reserves are increasing, and the list of commodities which the United Kingdom permits to be imported and exported freely without license is slowly growing and comprises some fairly significant products. There are signs of a decline in the degree of discrimination appearing in trade restrictions. However, convertibility may best be regarded as something which happens when equilibrium has been reached and not something which should be used to force a country toward equilibrium. Some argue that there is little to be said for partial convertibility, save as a first step toward full convertibility; that any steps should include gradual relaxation of dollar import controls as well as movements toward greater convertibility for non-residents. Although there is much to be said for making some progress wherever possible, others insist that the danger is far more that pressure for relaxations will force *de facto* convertibility before the surplus is large enough or the reserves adequate.

Because of these repercussions, because it seems likely that any too hurried new attempt to establish convertibility may be at most only partial and possibly need further support or continued quantitative restrictions on direct trade, and because it is doubtful whether the reserves are yet really adequate, there are many who retain doubts as to whether all the conditions precedent to an attempt at pound convertibility yet exist. But it is hoped that the attempt will be no more than postponed until conditions are fully favorable, and that the United Kingdom will continue to do what is possible to establish the conditions in which convertibility in a fairly extensive sense may be practicable.

Convertibility and EPU

The possible effects of sterling convertibility are not confined to the sterling area. It is likely to have very important repercussions upon the group of countries which at present enjoy a more limited convertibility through the EPU machinery. It is necessary to ask whether the possible damage to EPU convertibility is more than offset by the gains of a wider convertibility.

The essential of the EPU system, as has been shown above,

is that it ensures a high degree of convertibility and is associated with a fairly high degree of liberalization in the trade of an important group of countries. It is quite likely that a consequence of attempted world convertibility might be to diminish appreciably the extent of this regional convertibility and multilateralism. To indicate the possible chain of events, if some European currency is made convertible, there will be a strong incentive for the others to seek to earn surpluses in it; other European countries can obtain surpluses most easily by reducing their imports from that country; in self-defense, the country will reduce its purchases; by this process European trade will be contracted far below its present level. It can be said that, in practice, partial inconvertibility has been the foundation on which the increase of intra-European trade has been built. On any broader basis, there is danger that some of the weaker countries of Europe may lose the advantages of the EPU system without being able themselves to secure the advantages of fuller convertibility.

Another possible approach is suggested by those who believe that progress can better be made by taking the EPU system as the starting point and elaborating it to provide limited or complete convertibility with the dollar world. At present, the EPU system is designedly a regional system. It has certain limits and imperfections if regarded as a world system. It does not permit surpluses earned in Europe to be used to cover deficits outside Europe, except for trade with the sterling and franc areas. It has no built-in scheme for the sharing of dollars to correspond to the dollar pool of the sterling area, other than that inherent in its arrangements for fractional gold settlements. But the EPU system contains certain features, particularly for multilateral clearing, which the International Monetary Fund does not at present include, and is a possible nucleus for certain types of collective action in Europe which it would be a pity to destroy. It is by no means obvious that there will in the future be no necessity for the promotion of mutual exchanges within Europe by easy credit arrangements, such as the sterling area system provided before the war within a considerably more freely convertible world system than exists today. In the case of a collapse in dollar trade, the regional grouping might be of tremendous help in adjusting to the difficulties.

The proposal, omitting many details, would be to organize an EPU-sterling system on the principle of full monetary convertibility of balances and of rapid progress toward the general elimination of quantitative trade and exchange restrictions. Multilateral clearing and settlements would be made in dollars, and the capital fund would be supplemented by contributions from all its members. There might be limited automatic credit extension, but special assistance credits would be controlled by the Managing Board. Trade would ultimately be fully liberalized among members (except for limited special exceptions). Under the proposed system of settlements, there would be little or no monetary incentive to discriminate against non-members. The proponents of such a scheme would hope that the convertible account system would develop EPU as a major monetary center, attracting a portion at least of the monetary reserves of non-member countries (which would be given access to the clearing facilities of the Union through the opening of convertible accounts in their favor). British and other European facilities for the investment of reserves could regain in this manner some of the ground lost in the last forty years, while even American capital might find some advantages in using this channel for foreign investment.

CONVERTIBILITY AND THE IMF

Similarly, it is possible to envisage various steps toward wider convertibility under the aegis of the International Monetary Fund. In fact, the absence of any provisions for clearings or multilateral settlements, along with the failure to integrate closely trade and payments problems, are perhaps the most crucial deficiencies of the IMF in the long run. As it is now constituted, the Fund accepts no responsibility for maintaining such a system. Each country is supposed to restore and maintain convertibility of its currency but, if it does not, other members have no recourse to the Fund to convert their earnings in that country into means of settlement with other countries. The inconvertibility of any major currency leaves that country's creditors defenseless and may force them to make their own currencies inconvertible. A system of multilateral payments and settlements is the essence of convertibility, ensuring equal competition for all countries in all third markets.

Obviously, one should not be satisfied with regional arrangements, much as they can contribute. But any effort to develop a world-wide system is faced with difficulties arising from the disproportionate influence likely to be exercised on the operations by the United States balance of payments and by the difficulties involved in establishing long-term international committments. It is extremely difficult to create an effective forum for quick negotiation among fifty or more countries on the multiple issues involved in international monetary management.

At least one scheme has been proposed by a group of experts for using the IMF as a stabilizing force in the case of a serious decline in trade. The problem is a real one, and clearly the threat of a recession is a dominant element in the policy of many countries with respect to taking a chance on increasing convertibility. Even though such a scheme is far from adoption, there is much which can be done by analysis and appraisal and the insistence on the recognition of national responsibility. The IMF was predicated on the notion that no formal institution was needed for multilateral clearing—that speculation and arbitrage and private banking facilities would provide the necessary machinery once the basic obstacles had been cleared away. This may still be true, but it is also true that a very great part of the progress achieved in the postwar years has been made possible by cooperative action. In a very real sense, the IMF is not multilateral—it is concerned with each member country separately. It is not a collectively organized system fully protecting individual members against arbitrary actions and the use of bilateral bargaining power by any major country. And yet it is obvious that much can be achieved (as has been done by EPU) by joint and mutual action. It may be that convertibility will be achieved not so much by direct action on that problem alone as by the many separate and joint actions which can gradually break down the obstacles and build up the resources needed to permit trade and payments to move with greater freedom. To that end, the IMF has done and can do valiant service in providing technical assistance and advisory services to the member governments.

CHAPTER VIII

Economic Development and Capital Requirements

IT is difficult to talk briefly about the problems of economic development. Development relates to the economic life of a country, which in turn cannot be separated from its social and political structure, its economic resources, and its history. For the purposes of these discussions the point of central interest is the international flow of capital; this is, of course, related in many ways to economic development. However, each has aspects not directly related to the other. Foreign investment is important not only because it may facilitate economic development *per se*, but also because it may contribute to the solution of the dollar difficulties of western Europe and Japan and to their economic progress in general. Economic development, at the same time, is a process in which only one of the elements is the supply of foreign capital.

There is no specific agreement as to how one measures economic development, although the words convey a general sense. The most usual statistic used is income per head, but this is only a first approximation. It may be necessary to consider income distribution. (What does one do about per capita income in Kuwait with its $150 millions of oil royalties?) Also there are differences in the non-market sectors which are excluded from national product accounting. (Housewives' services have been estimated to amount to about 25 per cent of United States national income.) In either historical or international comparisons, the difference in the calculations arising from the fact that what are subsistence forms of economic activity in some countries are carried on in others in the market sector, bread-baking for example, gives a strong upward bias to the usual measures of economic progress based essentially on transactions. City-living has greatly increased specialization and the use of the market-place.

For a different reason, conventional measures may overstate the incomes of the more developed countries. Development involves a series of costs which should somehow be discounted if one is talking about welfare or progress. For the individual, this might include an item such as commuters' fares paid for going and coming from his home in the country to his job in the city. Similarly, government expenditures increase in ways which are not in themselves want-satisfying but become necessary in order to support the intricate structure of a highly industrialized society. Military expenditures raise another series of problems as they affect the usual measures of economic progress.

Another approach is that the test should be not so much the level which the country has reached according to some measure such as per capita national income, as the rate of change which is evident. From the point of view of minimizing discontent, it may be that the rate (or promise) of improvement is more important than the level achieved at any given moment. Measuring the rate of progress also raises difficult problems. It may be that a Dnieperstroi Dam creates a greater sense of advance than a five per cent increase in total agricultural output, although it may have much less immediate effect on national income. Nor is advance an adequate measure for all purposes. It may be that the index of discontent should be calculated in the form of a ratio of achievements (real or fancied) to expectations. However, development can be measured in capacity to produce. Some countries are so limited in resources that their outlook is bleak under any circumstances. But for most of the world, the problem is to establish a more rapid rate of development or even one showing some per capita gain.

Quite apart from these weaknesses in the notion of per capita income, there are added issues which arise as soon as one thinks in terms of the broader concept of welfare. Such considerations enter as old-age security, which has usually been taken account of in whatever may be the traditional way of life, perhaps through family organization; and the fear of loss of such arrangements may create one of the obstacles to change. Mortality rates, education, leisure, health, and comfortable routine are all elements which statisticians may ignore as outside the system of numbers and the market, but on which the people involved in the development process may place considerable importance. In some of these instances, it may well be that in the early stages of " development " things have to get worse for the ordinary man before any compensations appear.

Population and Development

Fundamental to any consideration of economic development is a consideration of population. In the first place, population provides labor and management as factors of production. In the second place, it provides the basis for calculating welfare per head (in some countries income per stomach might be more realistic). The population problem in the nineteenth century centered around the provision of manpower for production. Within recent years, it has become increasingly important on the consumption side, with the comparison of the rates of increase in national income and increase in population determining advance or retrogression.

For any given country, the rate of population change is the result of migration and of net natural increase. In the nineteenth century, much of the economic development took place in relatively sparsely settled areas where labor was a scarce commodity. Social and political factors (plus the tendency for reporting adventurers to exaggerate) led to a substantial international migration in the nineteenth century which played an important part in getting underway and continuing the economic developmental process. The emigrants from Britain, Ireland, and continental Europe were bearers of knowledge, skill, and culture. As entrepreneurs and workers, they complemented the capital that was also flowing to these new lands; their movement interacted with and reinforced the inflow of foreign capital.

Since 1914, a number of factors have contributed to reduce the flow of emigrants from Europe to other continents. The decline in the rate of population growth in western Europe together with its urbanization and industrialization, and the pressing back of the frontiers in most of the relatively under-populated parts of the world have reduced the fancied opportunity differential. Barriers have been interposed by the countries of immigration, both to restrict the total number of immigrants and to introduce selectivity and discrimination. In recent years, the cost barrier has been important—transport cost and the high cost of settlement. And here is one case where family ties, i. e., the insistence on taking the whole family, seem to be closer than before.

All of these factors are not likely to be temporary and would appear to indicate that the volume of international migration related to economic development will remain small. It is estimated that the efforts of the Intergovernmental Committee for European Migration aided 82,000 migrants during 1953. The leading receiving countries were Canada, Brazil, and Australia, with Canada taking more than one-half of the total. Important as this may be, it is small indeed in population terms.

There are other factors affecting the movement of peoples which have sometimes been adverse, at least in economic terms. Israel is perhaps a case in the postwar era where migration has stimulated development, although the fact of population doubling in five years has raised a staggering problem of absorption. But the refugee problem in Germany, little related to economic considerations, the population shift between India and Pakistan, and the return of Japanese from the Asian mainland to Japan—all represent major adjustment problems. And the closing of outlets, Italy to North Africa, India to South Africa, and Japan to the mainland, along with many lesser cases such as the Dutch to Indonesia and the British to Kenya, have also been adverse in their economic impact.

There is no doubt but that migration has been one of the important elements in economic development in the past. The immigrants, naturally selected for enterprise, extended the frontier. They brought with them skills and experience. They facilitated saving, in that the cost of producing and rearing the immigrant fell largely upon his country of origin. In some cases, they brought capital or claims with them. Their demands upon their new homeland were only in terms of opportunity. Because of these dynamic characteristics, immigrants, if they entered a country in sufficient number and its resource structure was sufficiently hospitable, built up for the home-country in particular, and for other advanced countries in lesser degree, an expanding market for fabricated products, services, and capital, as well as an expanding source of raw materials and produce for these same countries. And immigration frequently tended to dissolve customs and practices that had previously retarded technological and economic progress.

Today, the situation is quite different. It is possible that a significant volume of migration could be set in motion, but restrictions and barriers would have to be lowered and the costs would be tremendous. Its significance for both the relief and stimulation of population growth can easily be exaggerated though it might take the crest off the wave, if there is a wave. In most cases, it is likely that a given amount of capital can afford more relief from population pressure by increasing production in a country suffering such pressure than by removing people elsewhere.

The migration of management personnel and technicians should be rated as a special case. Even where there has not been heavy emigration from capital-exporting countries, the movement abroad of a sufficient number of nationals to manage foreign-owned property has usually occurred. Also, there are many recent instances where refugees with management or investor experience have played an important part in economic development in their new homelands.

One must therefore assume that, internationally speaking, we are in an age of labor immobility. This fact obviously has tremendous importance in at least three directions—first, it eliminates one of the elements which has contributed in the past to the rapid rate of economic development in some countries; second, other things being equal (which they are not), a relatively larger fraction of the world's internationally moving capital will tend in the long run to move into countries with large populations; and third, if labor cannot migrate, it will tend to move by proxy in the form of internationally-traded, relatively high labor-content products. In other words, the differences in labor costs resulting from unequal population distribution will tend to support wide differences in comparative costs as they relate to labor costs.

Today, those whose attention is focussed on migration are most apt to think of it in terms of relief for countries with surplus populations. Most of the countries eager for economic development are sufficiently populated to permit a cumulative developmental process to get under way without needing imported manpower. In fact, the problem for them is more often that of how to make progress in the face of a high rate of natural population increase.

Present rates of population growth would point to a doubling of the world's population in the next thirty-five years or so. The United States rate of population growth is now one of the highest in the world, for reasons which in large part are necessarily temporary. Decline in the age at marriage has accounted for about one-half the American baby boom, and the reduction in the relative number of childless and one-child families accounts for much of the rest. Present forecasts predict the United States population to number 190–210 millions by 1975. While not much population growth is taking place or is anticipated in western Europe, Russia and eastern Europe remain areas of high growth. The populations of various underdeveloped countries, some of which already are increasing more than 2 per cent per year, may be expected to grow at such rates or even higher in the immediate future.

With a birth rate generally over forty per thousand per annum and the possibility today, even when there is much poverty, of employing modern public health measures to cut mortality to and below twenty per thousand, the maintenance of a high net increase is obvious. Such rates could not long persist in the absence of economic development and in the face of continually increasing hardship, since then the margin of protection against crop failures and similar adverse events would be inadequate.

The death rate seems to be subject to fairly immediate influence from the application of modern health methods, but the birth rate is less flexible, being the outcome of attitudes and practices woven into the whole social context. High birth rates are requisite to the maintenance of populations subject to high mortality, and security in old age where there is no state or similar security system depends upon one's having had children who survive to provide this security. A decline in natality seems to be necessarily related to a major change of social texture (e. g., secular society, new and higher living standards, urbanization, greater educational opportunities, freedom of women, etc.) and a development of an alternative security system. These changes occurred in the West in association with conditions under which per capita income was enabled to rise faster than population, thereby reinforcing changes under way.

In view of the fact that these high rates of population growth increase the social and economic problems in countries already having large populations, it is increasingly recognized that a reduction in the rate of population growth is desirable (note current opinion in India and Japan). In fact, in the face of such population increases, it would be exceedingly difficult for the populations in question to improve their situations materially. As noted above, emigration offers little help since at most it could remove but a small fraction of natural increase. Only in the event that natality and mortality were already relatively low and falling (e. g., as in Italy and possibly in Japan and Puerto Rico) is there any likelihood that emigration would appreciably accelerate the advent of a relatively stationary population.

The solution therefore must be found through the reduction in natality. Even were an ideal contraceptive available, it is requisite that the social situation be one providing adequate motivation for its use. On the basis of past experience and of the fact that almost everything that reduces the birth rate at first reduces the death rate, it is not to be expected that natural increase will fall rapidly. However, there is a real relationship between the two. Reduction of infant mortality, for example, means a more rapid growth in the family, a greater pressure on the family's means of subsistence, a more rapid assurance of child-supported old-age security, and therefore a reduction in the pressure for additional births in the family.

Colonial systems usually endeavored to build upon the existing culture pattern. In general, they were conducive to population growth, as the histories of Java and Formosa show. In neither country was the culture of the people or their aspirations significantly changed, while the effectiveness of certain causes of mortality was reduced. As a result, population and income grew but neither economic improvement nor social change was sufficient to make for reduced natality. It would seem necessary for economic development to be exceedingly rapid and persuasive to effect a break through the Malthusian barrier. Only with a sustained rate of substantial improvement can one expect to see that cumulative developmental process in motion which might bring about the social transformation without which it is unlikely that natality will be sufficiently reduced. But here again emerges one of those difficult dilemmas —how to utilize any increase of income widely enough to get the birth rate down and at the same time increase saving and investment so that the economy will produce more income.

The impact of such rates of population increase on the demand for capital is tremendous. Merely in the maintenance of the existing per capita standards for housing, furnishings, utilities, etc., the requirement is substantial. Colin Clark has estimated that the present ratio between income-producing wealth and income is somewhere between three to one and five to one. Therefore, if population is increasing 1 per cent per year, additional savings of 3 to 5 per cent of the national income are required merely to maintain the per capita capital supply; and this rate becomes 6 to 10 per cent when a population is increasing by 2 per cent per year. Population growth thus becomes a substantial charge upon the capacity of the country to save, before the possibility of improving the average per capita level is even considered. Not only is the problem difficult for the underdeveloped countries, but it should at least be noted that the United States, the leading prospect for capital export, has also recorded a sudden significant increase in its own population growth, with not only a resulting increased requirement for capital but a consequent increase in the proportion of the dependent population to those of economically productive age.

There is at least one important caveat which must be added to the above analysis, depending as it does on the notion of the requirement for capital being proportioned to the population to maintain a given standard of living. The problem is in reality one of marginal increments. Housing requirements may indeed conform to a constant ratio, but what about roads or post offices? Perhaps the mere increase in population itself creates forces conducive to the increase in capital.

Exactly what element in the process of development brings about a decline in the birth rate is not clear. Such declines have accompanied rising per capita incomes in the past, but this association does not necessarily mean that the rise of per capita incomes is itself the cause. The cause may be some other element that has normally accompanied rising incomes in the complex of historical development processes, such as the growth of literacy or urbanization or industrialization. Further research into this question appears to be needed. If a clear answer could be obtained, it might be possible to devote special attention to the factors affecting the birth rate and thereby to break through the Malthusian barrier at an earlier stage and with less capital investment than would otherwise be required.

THE FACTORS IN DEVELOPMENT

Even though substantial development is needed merely to offset the population factor, it is obvious that much more rapid progress must be made if we hope actually to increase per capita incomes perceptibly and create that degree of change which will set a cumulative process in motion.

Economists have concerned themselves much more with problems of equilibrium than of growth. The process obviously is different in a leading than a following country. In the United Kingdom in the eighteenth century, manpower, innovation, and financing were all internal. All three items were imported in an important degree in Australia, Canada, and the United States. Japan and the Soviet Union provided manpower and most of their own financing, but borrowed technology heavily from other countries. To some extent, the countries late in the procession have one kind of advantage, they do not have to go through the error part of the trial and error formula; but the leader probably has an even greater advantage because of the cumulative processes involved whereby one thing leads to another. (One might argue that leadership carries the seeds of its own destruction. The records of the United Kingdom and Japan might be reviewed in this connection.)

Today, for most countries, economic growth is one of the most important objectives of policy, whether it be viewed from the aspect of economic welfare, of political stability, or of the military security of the free world. As will be discussed in more detail below, the provision of an adequate supply of capital cannot by itself do the job in the absence of technical knowledge, administrative capacity, enterprise, and willingness of large portions of the population in the underdeveloped countries to try out and to accept new techniques, new occupations, new work habits, and new modes of living. It is quite possible to argue, in fact, that the main impetus for development comes from factors other than capital. But it is equally true that these things will not suffice without adequate capital. Like all social growth, the processes of action, reaction, and counter-action are all extremely complicated, with multiple lines of causation.

The factors necessary for economic development may be classified under five heads: natural resources, population, investment capital, technology, and the spirit of enterprise. The spirit of enterprise may be defined as the desire to use economic resources as a means of increasing production rather than as a means of demonstrating one's position in society. In practice, this is almost synonymous with the idea that wealth is an instrument of change rather than of status. Some economic historians have concluded that enterprise and government are antithetical —that the way to encourage enterprise is to withdraw government restrictions. But this overemphasizes government. Actually, many elements contribute to a statically organized society, held stationary by the bonds of religion, culture, tradition, and social pattern. In fact, it is possible to have the spirit of enterprise as here defined quite apart from private ownership. Change and development may be sponsored by governments. In the United States, government played an important role in the development of transportation, not to mention the more recent explorations in the field of atomic power. In any case, the spirit of enterprise means that people accept change as a good thing, accept the breaking down of old social and political relations as part of the process of economic growth, and give appropriate rewards to those, in private life or in government, who help to bring about this change.

The factors of natural resources and population (in today's world with limited migration) are native to the country. Capital and technology, while they must come chiefly from domestic sources, can be given strong support from abroad at strategic points and times. The spirit of enterprise can also be engendered somewhat from abroad, but it must become the spirit of the nation. It is harder to acquire and is deep in the culture pattern. The central problem of economic development is how to achieve a dynamic growth and expansion process. Once this is under way, the process seems to be cumulative. But much too little is known about the process to draw many useful conclusions about it.

In those cases where there already was a well developed spirit of enterprise, as in the United States, the British Dominions, Japan, and to a limited degree in Latin America, foreign capital contributed in the early stages of development to the growth of public service facilities, such as canals, port facilities, railroads, and public utilities, and these developments all aided the cumulative process but certainly did not initiate it. At the other extreme in the economic enclave type of development (principally large-scale mining and plantation agriculture), local natural resources were utilized, but everything else including a labor force when necessary tended to be brought in from outside. Such enterprises often had little impact, at least directly, on the country involved. In other cases, where the concept of status is deeply inbred, resistance to change has been the social and economic keynote. Even where there has been substantial income resulting from some economic windfall, those who received it used it largely to increase personal consumption or hoards. To say that the spirit of enterprise was missing is merely to say that economic development was not taking place.

There is a very real tendency to associate capital closely with economic development, perhaps because capital supply appears to offer a controllable element on which to operate. However, there are grounds for skepticism as to the dominant place of additional capital in promoting development. Certainly, adding the income of new capital to a country's national income is not significant. If the amount saved per year were 10 per cent and the rate of return were 5 per cent, national income would rise only 0.5 per cent per year. If it is foreign capital, then payments must be made abroad which may eat up even this increase. Capital is therefore significant chiefly through multiplier action, when it increases the productivity of other factors or is associated with innovation, or both. Without these elements, return on capital will be low and little will happen. With innovation, it may be substantially higher and be able to attract capital for industrial uses away from real estate and hoarding. In many countries, considerable capital is available already which needs to be attracted into different uses.

Many of the underdeveloped countries have unused manpower, sometimes obvious as in the cities of India and sometimes taking the form of underemployment as in overpopulated agricultural areas. The objective of capital in an industrialized country is to be a labor-saving device, but in areas where there is surplus manpower, it must be a labor-using device. Thus irrigation, which adds to the arable land, may be a more desirable use of capital than farm tractors, which are essentially labor-saving, for labor saving may in turn create even greater problems for the country. Japan, for example, has competed successfully with the West by imitating Western products and making them by combining labor and capital in less labor-saving ways.

As a matter of history, it does not seem to have been a change in the supply of capital that started the industrial revolution, although the accumulation of capital was greatly promoted thereby. Actually, the development process in most countries has been cumulative. Most of the entrepreneurs have been able to expand out of profits and it was chiefly canal-building, railways and the like, which needed to find outside long-term capital (with an assist from local governments). The lesson of nineteenth century British experience in foreign investment seems to be that the big needs for capital in a developing country are for utilities. If these can be supplied from abroad, underdeveloped countries to a large degree can provide their own capital for the development of industry.

This points to the fact that, if all development rested on the use of increased amounts of capital, progress would inevitably be slow. The more that can be accomplished by changes in technique and by enterprise without large capital requirements, the more rapidly the underdeveloped countries can progress. This is not to say that the growth of capital is unrelated to economic progress. It is a safe generalization that more capital will be needed as the standard of living rises. But this does not put capital in the dominating position over development, since the line of causation generally runs the other way. With economic activity ready to be set in motion, capital may be needed to mobilize manpower. Working capital may be scarce both in real terms, materials, and even food, and in terms of finance, while labor may be un- or under-employed. Capital is also needed to catch up with the application of some forms of improved technology. However, even here, much can be done to increase productivity without much capital expenditure (e. g., agriculture). Innovation, or the introduction of previously known superior methods, can undoubtedly raise productivity to a considerable degree without net capital formation—for example, seed selection, crop rotation, plant layout, and the like.

CAPITAL REQUIREMENTS

It would be futile to treat in detail or to attempt careful estimates of the amounts of capital that are required. This would necessitate a translation of objectives into quantitative terms, a process which would involve many arbitrary judgments. Furthermore, there probably is no really meaningful single national figure, but rather a series of alternatives, just as there is for one's personal spending requirements. The capacity to utilize capital effectively is closely related to the other factors and the state of development within the country.

The capacity of a country to absorb foreign capital, given the terms on which capital is to be had and ignoring balance-of-payments problems, depends upon a number of circumstances. Among these the following may be emphasized: the relative magnitudes of the quantities of land, other natural resources, labor, and domestically-formed capital available for utilization with capital from abroad; the quality and training of the labor force, together with the degree of technological advancement characteristic of this labor force and its domestic capital equipment; the relative amount of enterprise or entrepreneurial leadership available either in the private or the government sector of the capital importing country; and the extent to which the imported capital may be accompanied by entrepreneurial and other skilled personnel capable of putting the imported capital to effective use. A country's capacity to absorb foreign capital therefore turns on the extent to which its technology improves, its supply of enterprise grows, its labor force and its stock of domestic capital increases in quantity and economic appropriateness, and its land and other natural resources become more accessible to use.

In most of the underdeveloped countries incomes barely meet basic consumption needs, with the result that the rate of current saving is low and cannot be greatly increased. At the same time, the amount of capital equipment used per head is so low that substantial additions to it frequently can bring about significant increases in output. In many countries there is a considerable flow of saving into unproductive uses (jewels and bullion), but in spite of any measures that might be taken to force saving into more productive channels, whether by appeal or by taxation, domestic capital formation will still be far short of the requirements for development. A ruthless dictatorship can depress consumption and increase investment to a considerably greater degree than a democratic form of government. However, there are countervailing economic losses and more important human costs which are disregarded by the dictators.

Similarly, some feel that much might be done by a more effective mobilization of labor. Where there are substantial numbers of unemployed in the home, it might seem that they could be put to work on capital projects. This may be true and certainly is a device used in the Soviet Union. However, it must be noted that the practical possibilities along this line are less than the figures of underemployment might suggest, unless one operates on a " slave-labor " basis: (1) family units that supported these " unemployed " could not be forced under any administratively feasible plan to transfer the released food resources to the community so this increased labor would be a real cost to the community until increased production from new sources was available; and (2) workers on construction consume substantially more than when unemployed at home.

It is not difficult to reach the conclusion, based largely upon general knowledge of present conditions and possibilities, that domestic capital resources are inadequate in the under-developed countries, that foreign capital is needed, and that the present rate of foreign investment and also the prospective rate under present policies, incentives, and conditions, is not enough to meet the requirements of rapid progress.

THE USES OF CAPITAL

Turning from the factors governing the amounts of capital required for development to the fields of investment, a number of issues arise of which some can be readily resolved but others must remain imponderable. It is worth looking in somewhat more detail at the various possible uses for capital, both of domestic and of foreign origin.

One possible classification is as follows: (a) social capital, such as educational equipment, health-producing instrumentalities, housing, and the like; (b) overhead capital, such as transport facilities of all sorts, public utilities, and communications facilities; and (c) capital devoted to primary production, manufacturing, and trade. It must be granted that such categories tend to overlap and that one cannot generalize too freely about any one category since its elements are not entirely homogeneous. It is clear that all these forms of investment are necessary for economic growth and that they require the application of resources, either to be saved from consumption within the country or to be borrowed from abroad.

It is not always easy to draw the line between these different uses for capital. When a company builds a factory, it may have to worry about related investments like roads, houses, schools, and hospitals. Some question can be raised with reference to any attempt to force capital into categories at all, at least in terms of any over-all planning. Within the normal range of choice, there is considerable substitutability especially over a period of time. If foreign capital meets certain needs, then domestic capital which otherwise might meet these needs will turn to other uses.

It should already be clear that the basic question is: what composition of investment is best adapted to triggering off a cumulative economic developmental process and at the same time setting in rapid motion a downward movement of natality and natural increase? The experience of the nineteenth century and perhaps that of Japan appear to suggest the importance on this double ground of overhead capital such as utilities, communications, etc. This sort of investment is essential to economic transformation and, being in rather large doses, is likely to produce some social transformation without stimulating natural increase.

Of like importance is social capital, a form of investment which initially played a minor role in nineteenth century development. This sort of investment is essential to the attraction of immigrants to underpopulated areas and the improvement of the native labor force, and is usually assigned a place of importance in the current development plans of all countries. While there is not yet any evaluated experience to go on, it appears that relatively heavy investment in social capital is especially well adapted to bringing about the social transformation of societies and a corresponding modernization of their prevailing standards, attitudes, and thought-ways. A decline in natality and natural increase would in turn appear to be consequential upon these changes. Accordingly, if the line of social causation runs as here indicated—and both detailed field and larger-scale studies should be undertaken to establish the argument—new emphasis must be placed upon a form of investment that has not been given much recognition in economic analysis, social capital, and this may require the expanding of existing institutions or the designing of new ones.

The fact is that in any developing economy, the great bulk of the domestic capital goes into social and overhead capital, including such investments as road-building, school houses, water and sanitation facilities, health facilities, and housing. Within this total, there is great opportunity for "veerage." A country can go slow on housing, for example, for as much as ten years. Since the requirements for industry are modest when compared with the totals, limited reductions in other forms of capital use can permit large industrial investment. The Soviet Union has obviously followed this pattern for several decades, and the United States, even with its large capital supply, has had to use special devices to direct capital in adequate amounts into some parts of the social sector such as housing.

A second set of issues relates to the problem of the pattern to be followed in development. If the comparative advantages call for diversified development, there is no issue between diversification and specialization. The dilemma appears when specialization seems to have the advantage. In practice, the issue tends to take the form of developing manufacturing (which is usually diversified) as against agriculture and mining which are more likely to be concentrated in a limited number of products. If such a development runs counter to comparative advantage, it may be practicable only by means of props or protective devices, subsidies or tariffs, for example.

Some observers look at history and conclude that industry is obviously more productive than agriculture, on the basis that countries with a high proportion of resources devoted to agriculture have low per capita incomes. But this disregards New Zealand, Australia, and Denmark as evidence. Upon examination, it is difficult to defend the proposition that a country with fertile land and other conditions favoring concentrated agricultural development would nevertheless have a higher output if it produced something else.

One suggestion frequently made is that more emphasis should be placed on food production for home consumption. It is believed that much can be done to increase agricultural output substantially with little additional capital outlay, by better seeds, fertilization, disease and insect control, and even by longer hoe handles. The problem here seems to be less one of knowing what should be done than of breaking through custom and tradition. Again, it appears to be a broader problem than just one of agricultural technology. There are too many illustrations of cases where excellent results were obtained under supervision, but where the new pattern reverted to the old custom-rooted type when the leadership was withdrawn. The community projects now being tried in India are efforts to achieve change on a much wider base than focussing solely on agricultural methods.

There is a good deal to be said for placing food production high on the agenda. A rapid expansion of food production will provide a basis for domestic savings, will minimize inflation, and is likely to improve the trade and payments situation. It is not likely to involve private foreign exploitation and a maximum result can be achieved with a minimum of capital. There evidently is less need for more research than for more application of existing knowledge.

As to mining, the objection frequently is that the greatest benefits go abroad and the yield to the underdeveloped country is not what it should be. This prejudice is based largely on the view that in the past, when such industries were largely foreign-owned, the countries in which they were situated gained little from their activities. This argument admits that the enterprise is economically worthy, but the objection is to the distribution of the proceeds. Even if true, this consideration is irrelevant to what countries with such resources should do now, because these countries have greater access to loan capital and in many cases greater political independence than they had before and therefore can encourage such production with greater control over its proceeds. In particular there is no basis for believing that the engagement of a large proportion of a country's resources in primary production is a cause of poverty. There is no reason in principle for avoiding development of primary production in countries where primary production enjoys a comparative advantage.

But having said so much in defense of specialization, it is necessary to note that these arguments do not mean that such countries should necessarily specialize in developing these forms of production to the exclusion of others. Specialization involves certain risks. Although the long-term prospects for the terms of trade are difficult to predict, it is clear that agricultural and industrial materials have wider amplitudes in short-term or cyclical price swings and total earnings from primary products are likely to be particularly unstable because the demand for them is derived.

In addition, it is worth noting that development should raise real income and consumer demand, and this demand will be distributed over a variety of products. If the developmental process has specialized on the production of a limited number of products, then much of the increase will probably have to be sold abroad. The outcome will depend on the prices at which the increased output can be sold abroad and the additional imports can be bought. This is a question of the marginal (not the average) terms of trade and involves important questions of price elasticities. All in all, dependence on one or even a few products is risky, and diversification reduces risks generally.

Capacity to Service Foreign Capital

It should be noted that the appropriate use of foreign capital does not depend upon, and in general should not be measured by, the direct balance-of-payments effects of the proposed capital inflow or the direct contribution that such capital makes to improving the balance of payments. In fact, foreign capital may appropriately be used when the investment projects with which it is immediately associated do not increase foreign exchange requirements directly, i. e., do not require foreign exchange to purchase foreign equipment, etc., needed to carry them out. Private foreign investment abroad often will exceed the actual foreign exchange requirements, but public lending agencies have been rather chary about loans to be used to purchase local currency. In such case, the capital inflow may take the form of consumers goods which may release resources within the country to work on the new project.

Investment projects within a country may affect foreign exchange resources indirectly by diverting resources, labor, materials, etc., from or into export activity or from or into import-competing industries. It may even affect the payments situation by generating an expansion of money incomes in the borrowing country, thereby increasing its demand for imports or attracting domestic activity away from export. However, in view of the fact that capital is somewhat fluid, the basic point is that while the foreign investment may define the use for the added resources which it makes available to the country and may mobilize resources for that particular purpose, it is only a small part of the total capital and payments flow and if it is limited to certain uses, there may be countervailing flows to other uses both within the country and in trade and payments.

Foreign financing may be appropriate for projects that make no direct contribution to the expansion of exports or the reduction of imports. The effect of the project on the country's total productivity is the sound economic criterion. This has been recognized, if only implicitly and indirectly, by the International Bank which in several countries is financing industrial development banks. These banks make loans for domestic projects on the basis of their contribution to productivity in general and not merely their " foreign exchange productivity." It may be argued that if foreign investment is confined to projects that contribute directly to foreign exchange earnings or savings, there is assurance that the capital will not be used for unproductive purposes and that this assurance would otherwise be harder to obtain. It should be recognized that this reason for the use of the balance-of-payments criterion is an administrative rather than a purely economic reason.

These economic considerations suggest that an excessive regard for direct balance-of-payments considerations may divert attention from other uses of capital that may be equally or more important for the development process. In this connection, it should be noted that balance-of-payments considerations seem to have played no significant role in the nineteenth century foreign investment process.

This conclusion does not mean that the future ability of underdeveloped countries to pay interest and amortization on capital is not an important consideration in determining the amounts that should be made available. But it does mean that future ability to service foreign capital without " undue " curtailment of domestic consumption or investment does not depend greatly upon the direct relation between the use of the foreign capital and the balance of payments. Foreign capital can be used in ways that will basically facilitate future payments of interest, dividends, and principal abroad without itself going directly into enterprises that earn or save foreign exchange. In the long run, the basic factors in a country's ability to service foreign obligations are its capacity and willingness to restrain its domestic use of resources below its total production, and its ability so to adapt its economy as to use a sufficient part of its resources in ways which will lead to the obtaining of foreign exchange.

It does not necessarily follow that there may not be serious problems associated with the servicing of foreign capital. The development of foreign exchange earnings in amounts sufficient to pay service charges when these exceed the inflow of new capital may require a reduction of real national income greater than the service charges themselves. This will be the case if the transfer requires a deterioration of the debtor country's terms of trade. However, the possibility of a serious deterioration in the terms of trade resulting from mounting service charges in the later stages of development is remote in time and uncertain of occurrence. It is doubtful that it should be a major consideration in connection with present policy, and it appears clear that it does not justify a reduction in objectives below what would otherwise be regarded as desirable.

The amount of capital investment in an underdeveloped country which is desirable is not confined to the amounts that can be profitable to the investor in a narrow monetary sense. Even on strictly economic grounds, i. e., apart from moral, political, and strategic considerations, an investment may be more productive than its immediate financial returns indicate. It may provide a country with social capital, e. g., improved education and health, which improve the productivity of the population. It may bring about a general expansion of economic activity and trade which increases real income over a wide area. It is probable that increments in each category of capital, social, overhead, and industrial, operate directly or indirectly to augment the output of goods and services, at least after a time. It must be admitted, however, that because increments in social capital operate relatively slowly to augment productivity and because their use is more amenable to public than to private exploitation, an influx of social capital from abroad, unless it comes in the form of grants or on very favorable interest and amortization terms, is more likely to eventuate in short-run exchange shortages which may intensify a country's payments problem. It is desirable, nonetheless, that a sufficiency of social capital, so highly essential to getting economies developed and ways of thought modernized, be available.

Overhead capital of foreign origin, though absolutely essential to a country's economic development and though speedily contributive (as a rule) to an economy's productive capacity, might also under certain conditions give rise to balance-of-payments problems. Almost by definition, neither social nor overhead investment produces things which contribute to meeting foreign payments. However, they do create conditions which make primary or industrial production more possible and less costly—for example, by increasing the supply of competent labor or by improving transportation to the coast. Under these improved circumstances, industrial investment of both domestic or foreign capital becomes more attractive and payments possibilities are improved.

FOREIGN CAPITAL FLOW AND PAYMENTS

In the previous section, the problem of servicing (and repaying) foreign capital was discussed from the point of view of the underdeveloped countries. Actually, there are at least three different ways in which foreign investment affects the pattern of the balance of payments. First is the initial investment which is usually related to some importation, either of capital goods which are related to the project or, where the foreign currency is immediately used to buy domestic currency, of whatever imports are eventually financed by the foreign currency. Second is the servicing of the investment along with possible amortization payments. Third is the fact that the investment may affect the income of the country. It may increase output more than the related servicing requires and may therefore expand foreign earnings by increased export or reduced import. Development may also affect the import side of the balance by increasing the requirement for raw materials, or more generally by the application of the propensity to import to a larger income base.

The effect of the initial investment depends in part upon what would happen if the foreign capital were not provided. To take the extreme case, if the shoe factory would not be built without foreign investment, then the shoe machinery which appears on the imports record would otherwise not have been there. The foreign investment permits the realization of a desire for a shoe factory, but it is not a correction to any previous imbalance—not a possible substitute for aid unless the aid itself took the form of the provision of shoe factories. However, given the present practice of screening private investments and planned government borrowing, the chances are that the new investment will be according to plan. Whether it actually would constitute resources added to those already available rather than a substitute for savings which could otherwise be utilized will depend upon the kind of adjustments made (or permitted) elsewhere in the economy. In the end, the effort to direct the particular investment may not change the pattern of development resulting from the use of all resources, foreign and domestic. Under all the circumstances, it is doubtful if increased foreign investment will itself act directly as a strong corrective factor in any existing " dollar shortage " situation for a particular country. It would be more apt to increase the purchases by the country correspondingly.

However, looking at the world picture, there seems to be little question that the trade and payments position of the western European countries and Japan could be improved by an expanded flow of capital to underdeveloped countries. The contribution of foreign investment to the alleviation of these difficulties has several aspects.

If devoted to developing production of raw materials and

food which western Europe and Japan now must import from the dollar area, foreign investment will enable these countries to substitute non-dollar imports and help them reduce their dollar deficits. This would help to solve one of the structural problems involved in achieving an equilibrium in the balance of payments without either United States aid, special quantitative controls, or difficult internal adjustments in the countries concerned. This long-run effect does not depend upon what country the capital comes from, since it results from the expansion of production for export in the capital-receiving country. In addition, increased supplies of these commodities even from dollar sources would also tend to benefit the payments positions of importing countries by reducing their import prices.

Insofar as the capital comes from the United States, it increases the supply of dollars in foreign lands and induces or permits increased purchases of foreign capital goods by the underdeveloped countries. This may provide at least the opportunity for some of the industrial countries to expand their dollar earnings, but it is important to note that these potentialities can be realized only if certain other conditions are met. As a minimum, the American foreign investment must not be " tied " to American goods, either legally or for other reasons, and the capital goods of western Europe and Japan must be able to compete successfully with those of the United States in the markets of the underdeveloped countries.

From the immediate point of view of the United States, the economic benefits of increased foreign investment except in raw materials are probably not of major importance. The continuous process of becoming a larger and larger creditor nation has embarrassing effects upon commercial policy. Any resulting improvement in the terms of trade or in the level of productivity or employment would be relatively small in relation to United States income. From the point of view of the United States, a possible but rather tenuous case can be made on grounds of terms of trade, but the much stronger case for expanded foreign investment rests primarily on political, strategic, and moral grounds.

CHAPTER IX

Factors Affecting Foreign Investment

THE SUPPLY OF DOMESTIC CAPITAL

IT is generally recognized that for any country the chief source of capital must lie in its own savings. There are, of course, various special cases where extremely promising natural resources have attracted large amounts of foreign capital for a particular purpose (Iran and Venezuela). But in most countries this is hardly a basis upon which economic development can be planned, and even in those countries where it can it represents a substantial capital inflow only in the early stages and thereafter the servicing of the investment may exceed new investment. There is the case of Canada which imported as much foreign capital in 1908–13 as it formed at home, but this was a short and unique period in Canadian history, a period which succeeded thirty years of little foreign investment. Similarly, the case of modern Israel, with her extraordinarily heavy capital importation, is an unique instance in modern history. In general, the available data indicate that the bulk of the increase in the capital investment of the advanced economies came out of domestic savings.

The supply of capital being provided domestically through voluntary saving and other means in the underdeveloped countries falls far short of what is required for their development and far below that which, in and after the nineteenth century, was domestically forthcoming in what are now developed or capital-exporting countries. The relevant data relating to capital formation in the underdeveloped countries are quite unsatisfactory. They would appear to indicate that both the national incomes from which savings can be made and the proportion saved are lower in the underdeveloped than the industrial countries. This is, of course, what one would expect. (One interesting form of domestic savings from the national income point of view is earnings on past foreign investments which are reinvested. Thus in 1952, American direct investments abroad earned $2,280 millions, took out $1,420 millions, and left the remaining $860 millions as increased equity.)

There is no doubt but that, as was indicated in the previous chapter, more can be done to mobilize capital into productive uses in these countries. In most of the countries (except of course the communal tribes) there are some individuals who are wealthy, usually because of their political position or the extensive ownership of land, and who might be a source of capital for developmental purposes.

The problem of how to strengthen or even establish channels of savings and investment is exceedingly important. At present, the tendency is to use the taxation channel as a means of directing income into investment purposes. Where, as in Russia, most of the national income flows through government hands, such a diversion can be carried out according to plan. Another possibility is inflation, but this has various other repercussions. However, the distinction between public and private saving and investment is not absolute—governments may save through budget surplus and debt repayment and thus indirectly encourage a shift from government securities to private investment. Furthermore, since much of investment is in housing, education, health, and public utilities, a large volume of government investment does not necessarily inhibit free enterprise in industry and trade. In fact, it may stimulate private enterprise by improving the background in which private investment can profitably be made.

The fundamental dilemma which an underdeveloped country faces is a most difficult one. To the extent that indigenous capital is mobilized, less may be available for maintaining the standard of living. In other words, consumption is already low and an increase in savings will in the short run depress it even further. Those in authority may be able to satisfy their constituents by promises of a brighter future (as in the Soviet Union), but they are bound to have difficulty in satisfying those who live in the present.

This points up again the importance of establishing the cumulative process of development. Once advance is under way, income is rising, and production is going up, it is easier to divert resources for development purposes—dividing an increase between consumption and investment is easier than lowering consumption in order to divert resources to capital formation.

Just what the relation of innovation is to the process of development is not clear, but it already has been suggested that it is one of the most important factors. It probably also has an intimate relationship with domestic capital accumulation. In the absence of much innovation, production techniques are likely to be backward, capital not very productive, and interest rates low. Under such circumstances, savings are not encouraged even if they are possible and such savings as exist are quite likely to go into hoarding rather than be attracted into productive investment. In turn, this hampers the process of innovation.

But when an economy has advanced to the industrial stage, innovation is made easy even without new investment. In such an economy, replacement of equipment is inevitable sooner or later, and for this purpose depreciation funds are accumulated as a cost of production. When new machinery is to be purchased, it will probably incorporate the latest technological developments and thus the application of new technology is provided for almost automatically. Although among industrial countries, industries, and individual business enterprises, there are decidedly different attitudes as to the speed with which machinery should be replaced, some doing much more patching and repairing than others, the fact remains that innovation does and can be applied in the advanced countries with much less new capital than is required in the underdeveloped countries.

There are various policy steps which a country can take to encourage domestic savings and productive investment. Most of these lie in the field of domestic action, but some fall in the area of foreign economic policy. Tariff and quota restrictions may be used to foster industrial development under the infant industry argument. However, these devices merely keep out foreign goods and do not actively push resources into the desired channels. Actually, they are more likely to serve to divert investment, by making certain industries relatively more attractive, than to increase the total development effort. Similarly, a restriction on the use of income for foreign purchase, say of luxuries, does not necessarily lead to its use in domestic productive investment. However, it is possible to lower the cost of foreign capital goods under a multiple-rate system or to reduce the obstacles thereto in the administration of trade controls. Once resources have been directed to the desired industries or economic areas, then commercial policies may be required to assure the success of the diversion.

THE TREND OF PRIVATE FOREIGN INVESTMENT

In the nineteenth and early twentieth centuries and particularly in the period 1870–1913, the foreign-capital requirements of the then underdeveloped countries were met largely out of the private savings of Britain and western Europe. A substantial part of these savings was transferred by the private international banking mechanism to the governments of borrowing countries or to business men operating in these countries. These transferred savings were looked upon as supplementing the domestic savings of the borrowing countries and thus as enabling the latter to import appreciably more machinery, equipment, skills, etc., from advanced countries than the borrowing countries could acquire through the sale abroad of raw materials and agricultural produce. One might have some difficulty proving that the foreign borrowing was specially responsible for railways, roads, factories, or any other specified additions to national wealth. The import surplus, for which foreign lending clearly was responsible in the sense that it would not otherwise have existed, may even have permitted consumption rather than capital formation to be maintained at a level above the country's unaided productive capacity. But whether immediately from domestic or foreign sources, there was a rapid and expanding use of capital.

Government foreign investment appeared only to a limited degree, notably where the governments of metropolitan countries made expenditures in their dependent areas supplementing the private savings flowing from abroad into these areas.

The order of magnitude of private international investment for the period 1870–1913 may be suggested through the translation of British experience into present-day American terms. In the course of this period Britain invested abroad about two-fifths of her savings, i. e., something like one-twentieth of her income. By 1913 her foreign investments, equal to nearly four-ninths of her home investments represented one-third of all European foreign investment and contributed one-tenth of her national income. Expressed in terms of the scale of the present day American economy, the equivalent would be an American foreign investment of about $600 billions yielding $30 billions a year income and growing something like $15 billions a year.[1]

British investment during 1870–1913 was largely in securities, the one-eighth which was in direct form being made up largely of investments in mines, plantations, and public utilities. A very large part of this investment (particularly in the United States) went into securities connected with the development of railways, with the result that frontiers were pushed back and vast areas were opened to low-cost food and raw material production. As of 1913, over 85 per cent of British foreign investment was in countries active in the export of primary materials. The investment itself moved abroad in response to the prospect of returns very little higher than those offered at home, proba-

[1] See A. Cairncross, *Home and Foreign Investment, 1870–1913* (London, 1953); also H. Feis, *Europe, The World's Banker, 1870–1914* (New Haven, 1930).

bly because the borrowing countries were largely Anglo-Saxon
in government, characterized by enterprise, and relatively rich
in resources. British investment, of which only about one-
fourth was contracted by foreign-government bodies, differed
from the French and the German in that more than one-half
of the latter was in government securities. Even so, much of
what went to governments and most of the foreign investments
of western Europe in non-governmental enterprises contributed
to economic development.

Since 1914 and more particularly since 1929, private capital
has not been flowing to underdeveloped and relatively capital-
short countries in a volume at all comparable to that experienced in the earlier period. World War I having cost Britain,
France, and Germany together $12–15 billions of their foreign
holdings, the United States emerged in 1919 as the world's
principal creditor nation, and its foreign investments increased
substantially during the twenties. More than half the American
privately-held foreign assets represented direct investment.
During the post-World War I decade, British foreign investment was at a rate about one-half that of the United States.
Lesser amounts flowed out of other west European countries.
Probably the total flow to the underdeveloped countries in the
twenties averaged something like $500 millions per year, an
amount considerably below (in real terms) that which Britain
alone invested annually in 1900–14.

The decade of the thirties which followed witnessed a decline in the American foreign investment position, the United
States actually experiencing a sizable net inflow of capital in
this interval. The fraction in direct investments, being less
easily liquidated, rose to about two-thirds. European foreign
investment was in relatively small volume, so the flow of foreign
investment in the thirties was negligible.

Since 1945, the flow of American private foreign investment
has been at a rate less than $1 billion a year, with most of it
taking the form of direct investment (not including reinvested
earnings). According to the balance-of-payments figures, net
direct private investments plus net other private long-term
investments were $963 millions in 1951 and $973 millions in

1952 (of which $118 millions went to international institutions). These figures represent less than one-third of 1 per cent of the national income of the United States and include capital flow to all sources. Nearly half of the 1952 outflow ($432 millions) went to Canada. Nor is the smallness of the American outflow compensated for by any sizable flows from other countries. In sum, therefore, post-1945 international, private, developmental investment is on a scale far below that experienced in earlier periods.

There are various reasons why current United States foreign investment is so low compared to national income. One obstacle is the situation in the United States itself, where the rate of return on capital is high. The investor is not attracted by foreign uses like irrigation or government borrowing where the rate of interest is comparatively low. He will invest in foreign situations where there is promise of a high return—oil, for example.

The absence of convertibility is also a formidable barrier to foreign investment, largely because of the fact that such investments normally depend on the transfer of interest and dividends through multilateral trade. The yield of British overseas investments was taken home largely in the form of an import balance from the United States or from other countries which purchased imports from the borrowing country. Again, oil has been an attractive foreign investment for the United States because even most soft-currency countries have been willing to pay for it in dollars or in goods which are absorbed directly by the United States market.

In addition, there are fears of existing or emerging policies in the borrowing country which interfere with the investment (and the investor) in various ways, perhaps limiting the profitability of the enterprise. These policies by the receiving country affect entrance, operation, and even the continuing existence and competitive position of the enterprise.

And finally, there is underlying political uncertainty which ranges all the way from the fear that some of the underdeveloped countries may adopt the Communist philosophy to the possibility of World War III.

OTHER FORMS OF FOREIGN CAPITAL FINANCING

The diminution experienced in the magnitude of the private international flow of capital relative to the need for it and to the level of world income has been offset in part by a number of international arrangements under which one or more governments finance or facilitate the financing of the outflow of capital. Most of this capital has gone for purposes not attractive to private investors, but which should serve to increase and improve the opportunities for private investment.

The International Bank for Reconstruction and Development began its operations in 1947. It is a lending institution using funds provided by governments and by borrowings in the private money market. With an authorized capital of $10 billions (of which slightly over $9 billions have been subscribed by member governments), it had committed itself by the middle of 1953 for $1.56 billions (about $500 millions for reconstruction and $1.06 billions for development). It has issued $556 millions of its own obligations, largely but not exclusively in the United States market. It has also sold bonds from its portfolio, $50 millions with its guarantee and $20 millions without recourse.

The International Bank operates chiefly on a project basis, having financed 250 projects in 30 countries. Since these projects involve outlays of $3.5 billions, the borrowing countries will initially be putting up more than the two-thirds of the total cost of the projects. Loans must be to governments or with government guarantee on a fairly long-term basis. The purposes of the loans may be roughly classified as:

	Millions
Reconstruction	$497
Electric Power	404
Transport and Communication	268
Agriculture and Forestry	150
Industry	149
General Development	92

The IBRD loans are usually designed to furnish the foreign exchange required for specific projects, and they must appear likely of repayment in the same currency. While the bulk of the Bank's loans have been made in dollars, it has made loans in other currencies as well. The prospects of repayment are exceedingly difficult to evaluate, since capacity to pay is related to the nature of the structure of the entire economy, as was discussed in the previous chapter. The Bank has taken the position that its loans will improve the debt-carrying capacity of borrowers so that their credit-worthiness would also improve and loans should be able to go on expanding faster than repayments are made. Nevertheless, the transfer burden is a part of the consideration. The interest rate charged is that which the bank must pay on its own bonds which have been sold on the market plus 1 per cent for reserve purposes for the first ten years plus .25 per cent as a fee.

The number of acceptable projects which are brought to the Bank is steadily increasing and the standards of the Bank have undoubtedly improved the nature of technical, financial, and economic planning in the various countries. Through its contacts with each country, it has had indirect effects on domestic measures taken to encourage economic development.

Limitations on the future activity of the Bank may come from inadequate funds, though as yet it has never had to turn down a loan for that reason, and from the fact that it must deal with governments. Nevertheless, it is expected that the annual rate of new lending (gross) will at least equal and probably somewhat exceed $250 millions a year.

The Export-Import Bank of Washington was organized in 1934 to finance American exports, particularly to Russia. In the immediate postwar years, it made over $2 billions of loans to European countries for relief and recovery purposes prior to the advent of the Marshall Plan. In fiscal 1948–49, repayments to it exceeded its disbursements, but since then the net outgo has ranged from $61 millions to slightly over $100 millions per year. Loans have been made to assist American exporters where the Bank participates with the exporter (Fords to Finland in which Ford and the Bank each extend part of the credit to the Finnish purchaser) and to foreign private purchasers of American products (cotton, tobacco, agricultural machinery, airplanes, locomotives, etc.). Loans have been made to subsidiaries of American enterprises operating abroad (American and Foreign Power in Brazil, Bethlehem Steel at Amapa, Republic Steel in Liberia). In recent years, a number of loans have been made to various types of borrowers for raw material development (manganese, uranium, tungsten, sulphur, nickel, iron ore). Lines of credit are sometimes extended to governments, effective as projects are approved (Indonesia, Israel, Yugoslavia, Columbia). In addition, the Bank performs other functions, handling guarantees under the ECA and MSA legislation, making loans to Spain under special Congressional mandate, and handling certain foreign loan arrangements for the Defense Production Authority.

There have been indications that the functions of the Bank are to be reduced, and the interest rate charged has been substantially increased. It may well be that the support of exports as such should be eliminated from its functions. However, it has been able to assist economic development (particularly by private enterprise) in some situations which would not be eligible for IBRD loans and in others where there was a special United States interest. Even if it were to continue former policies, its net contribution to economic development would probably not exceed $100 millions per year and under changed policies would be much less, if anything.

A somewhat different institutional approach is that of *The Colombo Plan*, approved in 1950 and involving most of the countries in Southeast Asia. It represents a series of individual national plans for a six-year period, based upon estimates of available local resources and the amounts of foreign capital needed to accomplish the programs plus some centralized machinery for providing technical assistance. Some indication of the nature of the programs and the sources of financing is given for the six-year period for four of the countries as follows:

	India	Pakistan	Ceylon	Malaya
	(Per cent of expenditure)			
Sector of Economy				
Agriculture	33	32	37	12
Transportation	38	20	22	20
Fuel & power	3	18	8	19
Industry	10	19	6	–
Social services	16	11	27	49
	(Millions of pounds sterling)			
Sources of Funds				
Total expenditure	1,379	280	102	107
Domestic finance	561	135	62	46
Sterling balances	211	16	19	–
Other external sources	607	129	41	61

As the table indicates, an appreciable part of the financing is scheduled to be done by drawing down blocked sterling balances. It is estimated that Canada, Australia, and New Zealand will contribute about £100 millions, and that perhaps £60 millions will come from the International Bank. This leaves nearly $2 billions (over the six years) to come from direct borrowing by governments in the market, assistance from the United States, or other sources.

The various national plans for the most part involve public investment in basic services, intended to provide favorable conditions for private investment at a later stage. The importance of the consolidated approach is not so much either in regional benefits or important international machinery as in the political and psychological advantage of having a program and in the technical assistance provided, particularly the administrative training and help which are being given under it to the Asian countries. For the purpose of this analysis, the Plan indicates something of the scale of development which these countries themselves think possible and the amount of external assistance which they feel they will require.

Another form of capital assistance which has been important during the postwar years is evidenced by the fact that the volume of exports from Europe to various markets forming part of the currency area of European countries has risen considerably and accounts for a large part of the total rise in the volume of western Europe's exports to outside areas. The metropolitan countries, on the basis of special monetary and political relationships, have made possible large exports from western Europe to their affiliated or dependent overseas territories through capital movements and military and civilian expenditure.

An estimate by the Economic Commission for Europe places the French public investments in overseas territories at $300–$400 millions annually, roughly one-half of this being in North Africa. For the United Kingdom, the release of sterling balances for India, Pakistan, Ceylon, and Iraq amounted to some £300 millions from the end of 1946 to the middle of 1952, while the outflow on private account to the overseas sterling area totalled little less than £1 billion during the same period. (The lion's share of this private flow apparently went to the Union of South Africa and Australia.) There has also been a considerable outflow of capital from Belgium to its overseas territories, and Switzerland has also been active in foreign investment.

It is impossible to make an estimate of the total volume of unrequited exports, and even if one could, not all of this would represent investment since some of the dependent areas have received substantial amounts of consumers' goods. Furthermore, a considerable part of this foreign flow was made possible by American aid which, instead of being specifically calculated to meet the domestic economic requirements of the United Kingdom or of France, took account of the necessity for them to finance capital exports overseas. However, it is clear that the United States and Canada have not been the sole sources of capital aid to underdeveloped countries, and it is not unlikely that Germany and Japan may also become important exporters of capital.

It is particularly difficult to sort out the assistance for economic development provided by the United States government in its various programs. Substantial amounts are made available for various purposes under the Point Four Program, which formerly embraced the Technical Cooperation Administration (TCA) and some of the activities of the Mutual Security Agency (MSA, which had replaced ECA), both of which recently became merged into the Foreign Operations Administration (FOA). These funds are used to finance technical and economic aid to underdeveloped countries in many parts of the world. The general dimensions of current United States grant aid for technical and economic assistance to underdeveloped areas (funds available) may be estimated at $433 millions as of fiscal year 1953 and $551 millions as of fiscal year 1954. Probably slightly over $100 millions per year are for technical assistance and related supplies.

In addition to the above amounts, the agricultural commodities shipped to underdeveloped areas under other legislation (India wheat loans, Pakistan wheat grant, and new surplus commodity disposal legislation) generate counterpart funds which can then be used for development purposes by the countries initially receiving the surplus commodities gratis or on a long-term loan basis. In general, the American aid program has to do with specific projects designed primarily to demonstrate better methods and to train people in their use. Capital grants are extended only if the project is needed urgently and cannot be otherwise financed, and then only for projects that designedly will be taken over by some agency in the beneficiary country. Special attention is given to projects which give promise of producing a trigger effect in the economic-developmental process. The major fields of activity have been agriculture, health, transportation, education, power, and public administration.

In addition to the programs related fairly directly to Point Four or stemming from the original Marshall Plan, there are various other elements in American postwar programs (like the port program in Monrovia, aid to the Philippines, or certain defense funds) which have in fact contributed to economic development, but it would require a most elaborate study to determine the appropriate amount to be so allocated.

It should be clear by this time that it is impossible to estimate either the demand or the present supply of foreign capital for economic development. The roughest sort of estimate, based upon public and private net capital flow internationally, might suggest a present flow of $3 billions per year. One could easily vary the figure widely by the way one defines what countries and what flows should be included. In fact, one United Nations study in 1950 put at not more than $1.5 billions the flow of capital into underdeveloped countries. Since the data suggest that relatively little of this capital outflow is moving into Asia and Africa, it is quite probable that these two continents are receiving far too little foreign capital for their development.

It is not enough in considering the relationship of capital to economic development to stop at this point. The actual volume of trade with the underdeveloped countries far exceeds the capital transactions. Since what they want the largest part of the foreign capital for is to buy goods and services abroad, it is obvious that expansion in their earning power will also permit them to buy more and pay for it in their current account. Thus, United States imports from the underdeveloped areas was $3.8 billions in 1949 and $5.7 in 1952. They were able to obtain from the United States in 1952 nearly $2 billions more for imports than in 1949. To be sure, the average price level of United States exports had risen 9 per cent (184 to 200), but this is only a rather slight offset in measuring the effect of the increased ability to purchase.

The interest of the underdeveloped countries should certainly lie in a high level of trade. And it is most to their advantage if the terms of trade are favorable. If they can increase their earnings without increasing the resources which they must use for the purpose, the situation is ideal from their point of view. As a matter of fact, the terms of trade have greatly improved since prewar, and even in 1952, compared with 1948 or 1949, had so shifted that an identical volume of goods exported from the underdeveloped countries to the United States was able to pay for an increased amount of American exports. Thus recent trends in both volume and value have substantially increased the resources available to the underdeveloped countries.

INCREASING PRIVATE FOREIGN INVESTMENT

Attention in the United States has focussed largely on the problem of increasing the flow of private investment. Consideration of this subject involves consideration of the policies of both capital-importing countries and capital-exporting countries and the bearing of world tensions on the confidence of investors.

As a practical matter, consideration of the policies of capital-importing countries affecting foreign private capital is in present circumstances largely a question of policies relating to direct (business) investment. The obstacles to United States portfolio investment appear to lie largely in disinterest in the United States (except as to Canada) arising from the recollection of past defaults, the uncertainties in international economic relations, and a reflection of world-wide political tensions. No new Latin American bonds, for example, have been publicly offered in the United States since World War II, and United States holdings of outstanding Latin American issues declined, principally through amortization and repatriation from an estimated $470 millions (face value) at the end of 1945 to $320 millions at the end of 1951. To be sure, the attitude of private investors or eligible institutional investors toward foreign portfolio investment might change if a sufficiently high yield were offered, but American yields are not niggardly and the potential capital-importing countries do not seem to be prepared to borrow at differentials high enough to offset the existing attitude.

Direct investment means essentially going into business in a foreign country. There has been considerable public discussion as to the factors which may be relevant. Many features of the economic, political, or social situation in a country are often cited as obstacles. So far as reference is made to such economic conditions as inadequate transport and communications facilities, unskilled labor supply, lack of power, insufficient housing and other facilities for foreign personnel, this amounts to saying that the lack of economic development in itself is a formidable obstacle to private investment. And even where the so-called obstacle is a matter of administrative regulation or policy, of which foreign exchange restriction is a notable example, this is often not a policy concerned with foreign investment as such but resulting from other policies and conditions at home and abroad which affect the country's economic position. Similarly, fiscal policies having a special incidence on foreign investments or restrictions connected with some national plan or program are often the result of internal considerations rather than of a deliberate policy defining the national attitude toward foreign investments.

The many elements which go to make up the " climate " have been widely discussed. Many of them raise costs and might be overcome if the yields were high enough. There are instances of considerable improvement in the investment climate during the past several years (Peru, Colombia, Mexico, India) and of deterioration (Bolivia, Guatemala, Iran). National policies determining the climate reflect apprehensions carried over from the past and aspirations associated with the acceleration of development. Countries want a rapid transfer of technical know-how and managerial responsibility, the training of domestic nationals, and the reinvestment of profits. They are biased against foreign investment in primary production and, particularly because of the quasimonopolistic position of many foreign enterprises, wish to appropriate to themselves a larger share of the gain than might accrue from the working of normal market forces. (The classic case of the carry-over of the stereotype of nineteenth century " imperialism " is the Brazilian fear that foreign capital will unfairly exploit Brazilian oil potentialities, so no exploitation at all takes place, local capital being either uninterested or inexperienced in the field and foreign capital forbidden.) Many officials are preoccupied, if not obsessed, with possible balance-of-payments difficulties and regard transfers of investment yields as competing with imports required by the investment programs they seek to carry out.

In many cases, the essential difficulty is uncertainty as to future policy, a condition not unknown even in more advanced countries. If these uncertainties can be reduced, even if the final set of policies were objectively less favorable than at present, it might eliminate fears which tend to envision the worst. But many of the difficulties lie outside the control of the underdeveloped countries and can only be removed as general political and economic conditions are stabilized.

If yields were sufficiently attractive, investment would probably take place despite most of the obstacles commonly encountered, but it is unlikely that yields will in fact turn out to be that generous, especially in industries producing manufactured goods for domestic consumption, since mass markets do not exist in underdeveloped areas. This type of investment is likely to come late in the development process when monetary and fiscal situations are stabilized, markets are broadened, local entrepreneurship emerges, and overhead facilities and social capital have been built up. Some of these developments may take a long time, and the possibilities of early expansion in the application of private capital (in terms of quantities measured in billions of dollars) are therefore limited.

One particular limitation is worth noting and that is the feeling (not always expressed) on the part of a power with colonial responsibilities that, having responsibility for the progress and the maturation of its colonies and especially having put in the social and overhead capital that has made these areas ripe for private capital investment, the opportunities for such investment should in the main be reserved to the parent country. Furthermore, it is likely to feel that it is better qualified to direct the character and pace of development of its colonies in such a way as to benefit the colony (not to mention its own interest). The postwar record, it should be noted, is one in which the parent countries have kept up the rate of investment in the colonies. However, it should also be noted that some colonial areas (e. g., the West Indies) are more and more making their own decisions on the source and nature of foreign investment for their development.

One interesting set of influences in this field stems from the effect of trade barriers. In many cases, it has seemed a better situation to a businessman to invest behind the barrier than to try to ship over it. Thus, a considerable part of American direct investment in manufacturing abroad since the war has been the result of the difficulties in the trade and payments fields. Where a market has been built up for a product in earlier years, the choice may be either to abandon it or engage in foreign production.

A number of proposals have been made that are designed to increase the flow of private capital to foreign countries. Obviously, the conditions under which economies operate in the underdeveloped country are of major importance—all those conditions which affect investment yields, risks, and the convertibility of funds. Some of these difficulties can be resolved in the traditional way by means of treaties. Undoubtedly, treaties can help but the difficulty of reaching agreement between two countries on the many subjects customarily included in such treaties has meant that, despite a major effort by the State Department, the number negotiated has been limited. Possibly if the effort were not made to cover so many matters in these treaties (a narrower treaty was negotiated with Ethiopia) , at least some of the obstacles could be eliminated. Recently a number of countries have seemed to be willing to enter into agreements with individual investors, giving them many of the assurances which they require. This is a hopeful sign and it may be that generalized policy positions may grow out of the experience of these individual cases.

Two other approaches have had considerable support. It would seem that part of these difficulties could be overcome by the extension of guarantees against certain of the risks, by the government for an appropriate fee. Although such a program relating to the two hazards of the transfer of funds and expropriation has been in existence under the European Recovery Program, little use has been made so far of the facilities available. The program has only recently been extended to new investment outside Europe. One reason given for its limited use is the unwillingness of business firms to disclose operating information to a government agency. Another difficulty is the fact that the present program does not provide for risk of loss from war or civil disorder. The program has not been popular with the business community, apparently because there is a feeling that it creates a sort of discrimination in favor of new investment (a potential group) as against old (an existing group) since the guarantees can be obtained only with respect to new capital investment.

It has also been proposed that existing tax incentives be increased. At the present time, American income taxes on income earned abroad may be reduced by the amount of income taxes paid in the country where the income is earned. Furthermore, corporations engaged in trade or business earning 95 per cent of their income from Western Hemisphere sources outside the United States are taxed at rates 14 percentage points below the regular corporate rate. One tax proposal is that the tax credit be allowed for all taxes paid abroad and not merely for income taxes. A second proposal is that business income earned abroad be completely exempt from United States income tax. How much either of these proposals would stimulate an increase of foreign investment beyond what would otherwise occur is uncertain. One consideration is that if United States taxes are reduced on these corporations, foreign taxes might be increased and the investor's position would be unchanged. Most underdeveloped countries have little incentive to enter into bilateral treaties with capital-exporting countries to eliminate double taxation, since they know that the United States already provides a tax credit so that if they increase or reduce certain of their taxes, United States taxes will increase or reduce accordingly and the investor will not have more favorable treatment. Furthermore, they are not particularly interested in easing the situation of their own nationals abroad or in encouraging the export of capital by their residents, but rather the contrary.

It is clear that, owing partly to their non-selective application, these proposals would involve a reduction of taxation on income from the much larger volume of capital that is already invested abroad and on income from capital that would be invested even without the additional tax incentives. It would affect investment in Canada as well as Indo-China and might not encourage any private investment to go into some of the areas with which the United States Government was particularly eager to cooperate in the development process. At the same time, these proposals share a defect common to more selective non-tax incentives in their tendency to reduce the pressure on foreign countries to improve the climate for investment. Finally, they raise questions which need not be discussed here of equity, consistency, and other basic aspects of general fiscal policy and even of public policy regarding the use of the tax machinery for incentive purposes.

Besides these two major tax proposals, technical changes have been urged in the system of crediting foreign taxes, and in the preferential tax treatment now given to corporations deriving 95 per cent of their income from other countries in the Western Hemisphere. Many of these proposals, although of lesser importance, appear to have merit.

It should also be noted that one of the difficulties in the development of direct foreign investment may be the unwillingness or inability of an investor to carry the entire burden of foreign operation. A number of recent important foreign private investments have been made with the assistance of government funds, particularly though not exclusively where new sources of raw materials are involved. This government aid to the private investor has taken the form of Export-Import Bank loans. Since these have carried a low rate of interest, they have pyramided the earnings, if any, for the equity investor in a very attractive way. This device might, of course, make almost any yield possible for the equity-holder.

In addition, it has been proposed by the United States

International Development Advisory Board in " Partners in Progress " and later by a United Nations Expert Committee that an International Finance Corporation be set up to assist in expanding the flow of private capital abroad in the form of equity investment. This proposed Corporation would be managed by the International Bank for Reconstruction and Development (which cannot itself make equity investments) and would secure its funds from governments. It would use these funds to help finance private productive undertakings abroad through equity participation and loans without government guarantees, providing financing in cases where a promising enterprise was held up because sufficient equity capital was not available to it.

IFC would limit itself to minority stock interests and would not accept management responsibility for the enterprises which it financed. The enterprises would enjoy no special immunities or status. Once the enterprise was successfully established, the IFC would seek to sell its interest to private investors who presumably were not willing to participate at earlier stages. It would then use the proceeds for another venture, in this way turning over its capital as rapidly as possible.

The proposal for IFC has been put forward frankly as an experiment and one which, even if successful, would probably not be a major element in the solution of the world's development problem, but it would be an additional support to the flow of private capital. Its sponsors argue that it will be helpful by providing capital, by bringing investment opportunities to the attention of investors, and by encouraging investors who may feel more confident of the nature of the project and its fair treatment if they are allied with an international institution.

It is believed that there are a considerable number of promising small and medium-sized investment opportunities abroad for which neither local nor foreign capital is presently available. The proposed IFC appears to be a promising way of meeting such needs. Since the need for capital is great and the prospects for its becoming available under present conditions are small, some experimentation with new institutions seems desirable. In the light of this situation, the arguments against trying the proposed IFC appear quite unconvincing. A proposal for a similar institution organized under private auspices also appears promising.

When all is said and done, however, it appears that much needs to be done to prepare the way for foreign private investment, except for the occasional attractive opportunity of the sort represented in the past by the enclave type of development. Even in the case of the World Bank, grant aid by the United States Government has sometimes prepared the way for its loans (Yugoslavia). Private capital cannot be expected to provide the preparatory investment, the social and overhead capital which is so basic. It will not provide the trigger which is needed for the cumulative process of development to begin to roll. Some countries are certainly ready for it today, but others are still too early in the stage of development. Of course, there are many exceptions and particular situations, but development must move ahead on a considerable scale and it needs more than erratic and specialized support.

Public Foreign Investment

While some expansion of private investment is probably attainable, especially if new institutional forms adapted to current conditions are developed, it appears unlikely that the expansion can be sufficient to provide the amount of capital or meet the type of capital needs that development requires. This is particularly true with respect to the very important requirements for social and overhead capital, the investments which prepare the way for the type of project which might be of interest to private investors. Capital for this purpose cannot be obtained from private sources, and it is in this area that governments have entered the field. Nor will an expansion in private foreign capital outflow greatly affect this sector of the capital requirements. It has already been pointed out that capital from government channels is already flowing to underdeveloped countries in considerable amount. But if it is not enough, one comes to such questions as the size and form of contributions that governments can make, whether their contributions to capital should take the form of grants or loans, and whether they should be administered through national or international organizations.

The case for making some capital available in the form of grants rests largely on the belief that development requires so much capital that if it all took the form of loans, the burden of interest and amortization charges would be greater than the underdeveloped countries could support or the creditor countries would admit within the expected patterns of international trade. In the nineteenth century, not only was the United Kingdom a great importer but there was a steady flow of investment out to offset the payments coming in. It may be argued that similarly the idea of there being danger of an intolerable burden on the future balances of payments is exaggerated, since if the loans are successful the proceeds of income and amortization will be reinvested and will therefore not have to be transferred, while if the loans are not successful there will be no repayment and therefore no payments burden.

It is doubtful if this argument can be pushed very far. As has been pointed out earlier, the success of a loan from the point of view of promoting development does not guarantee that it will be equally successful from a financial point of view, much less that it will be easily serviced in foreign currency, since ability to service loans also depends on the conditions and policies in both the borrowing and the lending country which affect their balances of payments. Attempts to repay, moreover, even when unsuccessful may put a strain on a country even though they do not appear as a burden in its historically recorded balance of payments. And if the payments must be made in dollars, the willingness of the United States to expand its imports may be the decisive factor.

It may be conceded that successful lending tends to induce more lending and that this would alleviate somewhat the balance-of-payments problem of the borrower. Clearly, however, it would not alleviate it as much as would the provision of funds in the form of grants. For a given volume of foreign capital, the burden on the balance of payments would be smaller the larger the element of grants or, to state the same point differently, for a given burden on the balance of payments, the use of grants would permit a larger or longer inflow of capital. On the other hand, it can be argued against the use of grants that because they are more likely than loans to be affected by political changes in the grantor country, their use endangers that continuity of the flow of funds which is required for any basic adjustment of resource patterns. Their use may also be objected to on the ground that it tempts the grantor to demand a political *quid pro quo*. Even if the grantor country makes no such demand, it is likely to be alleged and to create political difficulties between the two countries or within the receiving country. It is sometimes felt that grants engender resentment also by making the recipient country feel that it is the object of charity. And there is some question whether funds received on a grant basis will be as economically used by the recipient in the absence of outside supervision as will the proceeds of loans.

From the point of view of the country exporting the capital, it can be argued that its interest in making development funds available may be considerably greater than the prospective earnings therefrom and that therefore it might actually find it to its advantage to provide funds even on a grant basis. It can easily be argued that it was to the interest of the United Kingdom that the American railroads be built, even without return. The indirect benefits probably would have exceeded the loss of interest. The investing country gained from the shift in the terms of trade as food and raw materials became more plentiful. And a bigger world (measured in economic units) meant more trade for everybody.

These conflicting considerations make it difficult to come to a clear conclusion concerning the advisability of using grants on a substantial basis to provide capital for underdeveloped countries. It seems reasonably clear, however, that funds now available need to be supplemented by a significant volume of either grants or loans on a lower interest and longer-term amortization basis than can be obtained at present. The World Bank is proceeding with such loans as can be made on what might be described as " commercial " terms.

If funds are to be made available, the question arises whether they should be administered nationally or internationally. Several organs of the United Nations have considered the creation of an international development fund. Although this recommendation has met with no support on the part of the industrialized countries, a group of experts was asked to prepare a blueprint for such a fund on a hypothetical basis. The project is related to the statements made by two United States presidents, that if armament costs are lowered, more funds would be available for economic development.

There appears to be a role for an international development organization, provided its activities are properly coordinated with those of the International Bank. An international organization could exercise supervision over development programs in some countries where the United States, the chief supplier of capital, or other major powers might be unable to do so. Furthermore, the channeling of annual governmental contributions through an international organization would make it less probable that funds would be under as continual supervision of national legislatures than would be the case if funds were nationally administered and appropriations had to be voted each year after intensive and repeated examination of the administering officials.

Such a project raises great difficulties of organization, criteria, and procedures. One problem is particularly worthy of remark. The proposal for a World Development Fund made by the experts envisages an organization financed by annual contributions made on a voluntary basis by members and nonmembers of the United Nations. This method of getting funds (which has the Special Technical Assistance Fund as its precedent) was proposed to give contributors an opportunity to decide anew each year, after reviewing the Fund's activities, whether they wished to increase or decrease their contributions, and also allegedly to avoid straining countries that could not afford to contribute at particular times.

This feature of the proposal appears virtually certain to guarantee the failure of an international organization the members of which have different points of view regarding the subject of the organization's work. The largest contributors would completely dominate any organization set up on this basis since their possible withdrawal, even if not overtly threatened, would be ever present in the background. So long as the Fund could not depend upon contributions flowing in regularly, even its continued existence would always be in doubt. Under such circumstances the administrators could not assume continuity in their work.

As an alternative, it has been suggested that the World Development Fund be created to distribute grants of some fixed amount (possibly $2\frac{1}{2}$ billions a year) for social and overhead projects in underdeveloped countries. The funds would come from regular contributions proportional to the national incomes of the member countries. This suggestion appears to provide a better basis for an international organization than that proposed by the United Nations experts. (In the United States, no congress can bind a succeeding congress to make an appropriation, but the annual appropriation for the United Nations has become fairly automatic.)

It should be emphasized, however, that the problem of creating an organization is less important than a sincere recognition by all countries of their important mutual interests in accelerating the development of the underdeveloped countries and a realistic appreciation by all countries of the genuine obstacles to progress in development. Once these are attained, a practical basis for more rapid progress should not be hard to find.

There can be no question but that the economic and political policies in the underdeveloped countries will have a great bearing on the flow of capital. And improvement in the international economic scene in the areas of payments problems, monetary stability, and convertibility will also encourage foreign investment. But the fact remains that economic development itself cannot be exported and imported. Capital and technology can be made available but these are only ingredients and only part of the ingredients at that. In the last analysis, the responsibility for accelerating the developmental process must rest on the underdeveloped countries themselves.

CHAPTER X

Some Further Complications

The Complication of Domestic Policy

NO nation can determine its international economic policies apart from their relationship to its objectives in noneconomic fields. For example, it has already been noted several times that if military security is a dominant consideration at a particular period of time, then the use of resources will have to take that into account and other objectives become secondary. Similarly, noneconomic objectives in the international field may underlie a set of exceptional policies, as in the case of East-West trade.

However, even within the economic field, there can be and frequently is a real conflict between domestic and international objectives. It is not always easy to achieve compatibility among such domestic economic objectives as full employment, price stability, and economic progress, and it may be even more difficult to deal with them in ways which take the trade and payments situation into account. How much the policy-makers must take foreign economic relationships into account depends on the importance of foreign transactions to the economy, as indicated not only by the importance of foreign transactions in goods and services in relation to the gross national product but also by the adequacy of potential output from domestic resources in relation to the policy-makers' ideas of needs (consumption plus investment plus government expenditure). How difficult the problem of harmonization is (at least in concept if not in practice) will turn on the firmness of the various objectives, and the flexibility of the economy in making economic adjustments, particularly the degree of tie (if any) between money wages and the prices of internationally traded goods, either exported or imported.

If one examines the four possible cases (with no other complications considered), where over-full employment or unemployment coexists with a balance-of-payments deficit or a balance-of-payments surplus and one considers the appropriate use of monetary and fiscal measures, it is clear that the case of over-full employment with a balance-of-payments deficit would call for deflationary action. There is no policy incompatibility in the case where demand is high for both domestic and foreign goods, except for the possibility that the steps to reduce demand may not work equally in both situations and the effort required to correct the foreign situation might reduce the level of employment at home by more than a tolerable degree. Similarly, if the situation is dominated by less than a full use of resources, so that there is unemployment at home and if at the same time there is a surplus in the balance of payments, then measures taken to increase demand would assist in improving both situations.

But the problem becomes more difficult if unemployment is associated with a balance-of-payments deficit. Efforts to expand demand at home would presumably also increase the demand for foreign goods and possibly reduce further the volume of exports. Under such circumstances, the domestic problem would have been dealt with at the expense of the foreign, or the effort to correct the foreign imbalance would further increase unemployment at home. In such a case, the objective would presumably be to adopt a policy which would increase domestic demand, i. e., employment, and not increase the demand for foreign goods. One way of shifting the foreign and domestic impact of monetary measures either directed at inflation or deflation (without applying added trade restrictions) is by exchange rate adjustment. The effectiveness of this instrument is related to the flexibility of the processes of economic adjustment within the economy. In fact, as has already been pointed out, automatic price-wage ties appear to be one of the most serious sources of difficulty in shifting demand between the foreign and domestic areas by monetary measures and exchange rate adjustments.

Where both domestic and foreign relationships play an important part in the economic life of the country, the priorities among types of action from the point of view of short periods obviously depend upon judgment as to the temporary or permanent character of the factors which have created the problems, the state of the reserves or the willingness to restrict foreign trade by quantitative controls, and the sensitivity and reactions of the public to price rises and their willingness to tolerate given degrees of unemployment. Given the basic political necessity of governments, it is not unlikely that employment will be given priority, and controls of one kind or another will be utilized to force whatever adjustment is needed in the international sphere. If such action is taken without regard for employment conditions in other countries, increases which tend to shift unemployment to other countries may induce retaliation or reduction in foreign demand due to the changed situation in the other country quite apart from conscious retaliation, and all may be damaged.

The above discussion has been greatly oversimplified and many other factors may make particular situations easier or more difficult to handle. The point which needs to be kept in mind is the very real possibility of conflict between the measures which are directed toward the goal of full employment (as that may be defined in any particular country) and those intended to achieve an expanding, or at least a balanced, trade and payments situation.

But domestic policy does not come into conflict with international policy only in connection with such pervasive problems as the achieving and maintenance of full employment. There are many more limited domestic objectives which necessitate special treatment in the international field. One of the most important illustrations of this is the case of agriculture. Some would explain its special position by the political strength of farmers in many countries. Others would emphasize the basic importance of food to an economy and the desire to be self-sufficient in this field or at least to ease the payments situation. Still others would defend special farm programs on the ground that market forces do not work satisfactorily in this area and that farmers are usually hurt by depressions much more than any other important group in society.

There is a paradoxical contrast between the attempts of many industrial countries to maintain or expand their agriculture and the attempts of some primary producing countries to contract agriculture and expand industry, an apparent conflict which may be reconciled by the common objectives of diversification and self-sufficiency. The effort to aid agriculture frequently takes the form of direct assistance and subsidy. In the United States the current agricultural program relies upon maintaining internal agricultural prices in relation to parity, which generally means supporting agricultural prices above the world level. Such a program encourages domestic production, since farm income will rise or fall according to the quantity produced, if prices are inflexible. For a food-importing country, which is trying to encourage domestic agriculture by high prices, import controls must be established to prevent the high prices from attracting foreign supplies unduly and putting too great a strain on the support machinery. For an exporting country, the domestic market is limited to that which can be sold at the support price level (except as separable markets like school-lunch programs can be found). Therefore some form of subsidy or two-price system must be used to move the surplus into export at the lower price level of the world market, or surpluses must be accumulated in government hands (to which process there is a limit), or steps must be taken to restrict production, a course which tends to negate the original objective not of maintaining prices but of supporting farm income (the product of prices times production).

The chief alternative which has been suggested is to allow prices to find their own level and to maintain farm incomes by some other device. This of course suggests the possibility that if incomes are assured quite independently of output and if prices are allowed to fall, incentives to produce or even to improve efficiency might be weakened, and various formulae have been suggested to meet this difficulty. Strictly from the viewpoint of international economic policy, the recognition of the world price would ease the situation greatly, eliminating charges of dumping, subsidy, or unfair competition. Production about the world would be more likely to develop in the more efficient areas and imports and exports would not need special treatment to prevent their being determined by the high domestic prices.

The problem of agricultural policy is not unlike that of any industry where there is an effort to give it a protected position, which really means erecting barriers of one sort or another to protect it from the forces of competition. If it is to be on a healthy basis without special supports, it must be in the proper balance with other types of economic activity. It may be that so far as the United States is concerned, the agricultural situation will be largely corrected in the near future by the rapid increase in population. Were it not for this probability and the obvious political considerations, it might be argued that since subsidies are already involved in protecting agricultural income, it might be better in terms of long-run effects to use such subsidies to help more farmers off the farm.

In many other countries, including most in western Europe, the problem is quite the opposite—how to encourage and stimulate domestic agricultural production in order to reduce their dependence on food imports, which they may not have the foreign exchange to buy. In the United Kingdom, for example, less than one-half of its food consumption is covered by home-grown food and feed. Many Europeans would argue that even though the major part of European agriculture is noncompetitive and of high cost in relation to overseas imports, this is not a sufficient argument against attempts to increase production so long as the manpower now employed in agriculture cannot be transferred to other areas of the world or to other branches of the European economy. This position is of course strengthened by the balance-of-payments situation. Thus domcstic policy and the possibility of adjustment in the international economic situation are thoroughly interrelated.

One further complication related to special interests needs to be noted, and that is that governments are not the only agencies which interfere with processes of economic adjustment and change. Private business arrangements of one sort or another may exercise substantial influence without dependence upon government sanctions. Private cartel arrangements may restrict production, allocate foreign markets, or maintain prices. There has been a notable increase in public concern over these private monopolistic arrangements in a number of countries, as evidenced by legislation though often limited to investigation, and the fact that the United Nations has devoted considerable time and energy to the problem. However, the United States still stands out as the only country where private actions " in restraint of trade " are clearly contrary to public policy. While the basis of the European Coal and Steel Community is to increase the degree of competition within the area, the private producers are still free to trade outside the area under cartel-like arrangements and are doing so at least with respect to price-fixing. In both Germany and Japan, there are vigorous proponents of the idea that their economic prospects would be improved if something like the old private concentration of economic power could be re-established.

These arrangements not only may affect the volume and direction of trade, but they also have their influence on foreign investment, particularly in the field of manufacturing and trade. The foreign entrant may have a problem in making a tolerable peace with the domestic competitors in the same industry, and the difficulties are sometimes such as to prevent the foreign investment from taking place. In at least one instance an American company was allowed to have a branch plant in a country on condition that it not sell its product in the country. There is, of course, no way of evaluating the significance of private arrangements in influencing economic behavior directly. Undoubtedly, they also have a hand in the development and application of government policies as well.

INTERNATIONAL ORGANIZATIONS

While international economic policies of countries are limited on the one hand by domestic considerations, they are affected on the other by international organizations. To be sure, the transfer of sovereignty has been slight indeed, but there can be little doubt but that international organizations have achieved a new importance since the war. It seems clear that a set of common policies requiring cooperative action in dealing with common problems is sometimes needed among governments (as well as within them), and that international organizations can aid in attaining that end. Underlying all consideration of the form and character of international institutions must be the recognition of the importance of the personalities included, both the representatives of governments and the officials and secretariat. There is no magic in international organizations *per se*.

A first category of possible functions for international organizations is the development of new lines of policy, but there are major difficulties which limit their usefulness for this purpose. In this connection, it is important to remember that individual governments do not always arrive easily at clear-cut policy decisions. At least one significant factor is the rank and status in their respective governments of the various national representatives to such organizations. This of course varies from time to time and from government to government and is undoubtedly related to the interest and concern about the actions which might be taken by the organization. With the increasing number of international meetings, it is difficult for countries to be represented by their top-flight policy men. Representatives may be technicians who frequently cannot speak with authority for their governments, or they may be generalists who are not fully competent. And those attending may be hampered either by too detailed instructions or the complete absence of them.

Once they are there, the consideration by the assembled group of representatives may be distorted by bloc obligations, for there is a tendency to develop bloc views and bloc political techniques. This is particularly limiting if the blocs are not temporary in character and addressed to specific issues, but become entrenched groups committed to vote together on wholly unrelated issues. Furthermore, there is another difficulty if the discussions are public, since positions are then likely to be adapted to foreign or domestic public consumption at the moment.

International organizations are frequently able to contribute to the development of coordinated international policy at the second stage. If carefully prepared by a small group of countries or by the secretariat, the organization may serve as a means of exploring and extending an agreement. The forum of the organization can be used to educate national representatives generally about the proposal, to determine the extent of agreement, and to weigh possible modifications which may be necessary to give the proposal general acceptability.

A second broad function is that of obtaining and maintaining national commitments to an agreed policy. This is likely to be an important objective, particularly at the start. Obviously, it is desirable to make international economic life more orderly, just as legal systems create a degree of order within nations. There are two reservations which must be made. First, such agreements may not be a real achievement at all, being the lowest common denominator or an apparent agreement via ambiguity. Second, there is the possible danger in a complicated situation, of transferring the emphasis of the organization from concern about a set of problems to concern over the application or interpretation of a particular set of articles or phrases. On the other hand, it may be possible to obtain international commitments when the problems are not acute, and this is very much to the good if the commitments are relevant to some problem in the form in which it finally appears. Also, in a world of nationalism, it is doubtful if legislative bodies would be willing to accept general obligations rather than fairly specific ones.

The third area is that of the operation or carrying out of agreed policy. Many of the more successful agencies operate in

fields where it is clear that international action is essential—
the International Postal Union, the Commission on Narcotics,
and the Safety at Sea Convention, for example. There are many
situations calling for joint participation or cooperative action
such as postwar trade agreement negotiation and interpretation
in GATT, recommended allocation of strategic items in
NATO, and the development of a common program for western Europe in the OEEC. There is also the function of interpretation—the provision of equity. And there are situations
which can best be dealt with by the use of international prestige. This may take the form of providing a non-nationalist
sponsorship for some type of activity or of achieving enforcement by group pressure.

Finally, there is the function of description, measurement,
diagnosis, and analysis of the problems within a particular field.
This is the area in which the international secretariat can per-
form a valuable service. As to the functioning of the secretariat,
this is a matter on which it is exceedingly difficult to generalize. How positive a force it should be seems to be a matter both
of personalities and of the functions performed by the organization. When its responsibilities are fairly definite and more or
less administrative, the secretariat probably must play an active
part. If the functions of the organization are at the policy level
with major political overtones, an aggressive secretariat can
cause positive harm since it can operate with no real policy
responsibility, although *ad hoc* committees have proved to be
an excellent device for developing a general concept on occasion. The basic responsibility of any secretariat certainly is to
make the organization work and that may involve providing
facts and pointing up issues, but the organization is essentially
an organization of governments.

There is doubt by some as to whether most of the present
international organizations are really serving a useful function
or making a contribution commensurate with their cost and
the drain which staffing them has put on national personnel,
but it is difficult to find adequate criteria for such an evaluation. The extensive development of these organizations is so
new that most analysts would center their attention on how to

make the organizations work better, rather than worry too much about the present over-all structure, burdensome as it may be.

It seems clear that there is not enough coordination among the various organizations themselves, although a valiant and only partially successful effort has been made to correlate the activities of the many different specialized agencies in the field of technical assistance. And the trade and payments problem suffers from the differing nature and status of the IMF and the GATT. Thus the Fund, in studying the economic situation of all its member countries who were in balance-of-payments difficulties, had to take their commercial policy for granted and determine whether or not balance-of-payments difficulties did in fact exist. Its findings concerning the existence of such balance-of-payments difficulties were conclusive in GATT. And GATT in turn considered whether or not, on the basis of these premises, the country could properly pursue discriminatory trade policies. Each organization could deal only with a phase of the problem and neither could hold the country to account for its over-all policy.

As to dealing with trade and payments in one organization, or at least their coordination through a common managing board, the OEEC–EPU experience supports such an idea. However, the fact is that in many governments, these two subjects are similarly handled by separate bodies with separate groups of technicians. At least, added and stronger forms of coordination need to be developed. Certainly, these problems must be brought closer together. The complaint can also be made that a major difficulty is national confusion of policy, that governments do not have reconciled views within themselves. Nor can one hope for complete clarity in national policies. Valid objectives may be in conflict and priorities will be altered from time to time as problems, personalities, and policies change in the country concerned. Probably the number of international agencies is partially a manifestation of this situation, and raising the conflict of specialists to the international level suggests the possibility of confusion twice compounded. On the other hand, the definition of international issues by international agencies can serve to force countries to make policy decisions.

THE NEED FOR ACTION

The foregoing pages have presented a complicated picture. International economic policy cannot be abstracted from other kinds of policy, both non-economic and economic. And the many elements within the international economic field are themselves interrelated and interdependent. It may be argued, given the manner in which countries attempt to protect their payments situations, the possible adverse effects of constructive foreign economic policies on their domestic price levels and employment, and the accretion of vested interests opposed to change as time elapses, that the present international disequilibrium will tend to be self-perpetuating. Furthermore, there are various vicious circles which seem to set limits to progress. For example, the lack of convertibility tends to distort the pattern of trade and investment and the present distortion of trade and investment patterns makes convertibility impossible.

The above statement is based upon much too static a picture of the world economic situation. The changes which have occurred since the war have been tremendous and there are dynamic forces at work which will force further changes. So far as the United States is concerned, such problems as the continuation of aid programs, the persistent demand by certain groups for increased protection, and the accumulating agricultural surpluses make inaction impossible. In fact, very few countries, if any, are content with the present situation, and even if they do not initiate action themselves, they at least must react to disturbing forces from abroad. And many of these forces, economic development for instance, cannot help but lead to new international trade and payments patterns.

Sometimes, decisions are made which are clearly of major importance—the launching of the Marshall Plan, the establishment of EPU, the sterling area reaction to the crisis of 1949. But there also is the continual stream of daily decisions usually related to specific limited situations which in the long run determine much of the total international behavior pattern.

These decisions often cannot be postponed. Failure to act may be just as decisive as action.

Unfortunately, there does not seem to be any single act of magic which will put the disorder straight. Rather, there must be a converging set of actions which will work in the direction of putting international relations on a more balanced, more stable, and freer basis. Truly, this is a transition period, although there may be some question as to the goal toward which the world is in transit. The goal is certainly not as clear in full outline as one might like, recognizing the heterogeneity of nations and of their individual objectives (not to mention the extent to which there are disagreements among economists themselves), but the general direction in which progress lies is somewhat clearer.

This situation might be regarded by some as a reason for taking as little action as possible—reacting when necessary but never assuming a positive position. This is not a necessary conclusion. There is in the first place a great need for much more understanding by everyone—by the experts whose expertness includes an awareness of the areas in which they are uncertain, and also by politicians and the public who are too likely to seize upon overly simple solutions. But even within the present degree of knowledge, some types of action would clearly be beneficial, and others can be said to be more likely to help than to injure. Most countries now have much more freedom of choice than they had in the immediate postwar years when shortages dominated the picture so completely, so it is more necessary that policies be concerted in the right direction. The world is closer to convertibility and more liberal policies than at any time since the war; few countries now have tremendous deficits in their trade and payments situation, although less can be said as to the improvement in the flow of capital. Although the present situation was achieved in part through restrictions, they are probably less and less the economically effective condition of present balance, though how much the remaining pent-up demand may be, no one can say. Increased output and monetary policy largely account for this progress and have taken much of the force out of quantitative interventions. It is not inordinately optimistic to suggest that if the trends of improvement should continue, and additional opportunities to earn dollars should be afforded rather than the reverse, it would not be long before the structural adjustments would have been made which are needed for payments equilibrium and convertibility. However, the fact that United States military spending abroad recently has been more than the increase in world reserves, shows how tenuous the balance is which has been achieved.

The part which the United States will play in shaping the future cannot help but be important. Given its economic position in the world, its actions or inactions are certain to affect the problems and policies of other countries. Most traditional economic analysis tends to establish the comfortable presumption that there is an inherent tendency toward equilibrium and that interference is likely to be harmful. But this assumes a freedom and flexibility for adjustment to take place both domestically and internationally, which is far from the reality of today, and today's actions must be taken in today's world. The United States will exercise its position constructively if it seeks the reduction of restrictions, but even more, if it contributes to the correction of the situations which have made the restrictions necessary. The world is far from having reached its economic potential.

American foreign economic policy will not be judged solely in terms of its economic impact and economic implications. The effort is made by unfriendly persons to create a picture of the United States as a country exclusively concerned with materialistic accumulation, using and exploiting her friends. It is easy to challenge this concept by pointing to the record. The record is a living one, being added to day by day. Decisions are being made which affect the conditions of living in many countries. These actions cannot be hidden, and the fact remains that economic foreign policy is one of the important elements which create the symbol in men's minds everywhere representing the United States to them.

Index

velopment, 192; and foreign in- vestment, 30, 178; prewar, 8; recent trends, 10; stabilizing, 98
Theory, economic and practice, 21
Third countries, and convertibility, 146; competition in, 66, 112
Thorp, Willard L., xi
Tied loans, 174, 178
Trade agreements, bilateral, 81
Trade barriers, and convertibility, 133; and foreign investment, 196; reduction by OEEC, 83
Trade and payments situation, *see* Balance of payments
Trade, and convertibility, 128; and position of underdeveloped countries, 192; declining proportion of manufactures, 58; expansion of, 55; fluctuations, 19; liberalization, 80; manufactures, history, 55
Trade expansion, an objective, 17
Trade, Not Aid, 34; adjustment to by individual countries, 36; shift in incidence, 36
Trade patterns, and eastern Europe, 60; shifts, 58
Trade trends, prewar, 7; possible collapse, 17; postwar, 3
Transition period, 69, 106
Treaties, commercial, 196
Triffin, Robert, x, xi

Underdeveloped areas, 154; problems of, 12; savings, 30; supply of domestic capital, 179
Unemployment and tariff reductions, 93
United Kingdom, changed payments position, 129; convertibility proposal, 146; devaluation of 1949, 68, 110; foreign investment record, 182; imports, 55; nineteenth century position, 76; terms

of trade, 65; terms of trade, prewar, 8
United Nations Economic Commission for Europe, 27, 61, 88, 190
United Nations Relief and Rehabilitation Administration, 26, 70
United States, assistance for economic development, 190; benefits of foreign investment, 178; capital requirements, 162; commercial policy, 89; competition in non-European markets, 67; effect of, recessions, 143; extraordinary dollar payments, 35; foreign investment record, 184; foreign aid programs, 25; importance of trade, 6, 20; increases in imports, 91; population growth, 159; postwar trade trends, 3; productivity, adjustment to, 63; share in world trade, 7, in manufactures, 56; tariff policy, 89; proposals for changes in, 96; tax incentives, foreign investment, 197; terms of trade, 65; trade development, 77
Unrequited exports, 190
USSR, trade policy, 11

Venezuela, multiple rate systems, 115
Vernon, Raymond, x, xi
Vested interests and controls, 49

Wages, prices, and adjustment, 45, 108, 208; and productivity, 62
Welfare in development, 156
Western Europe, postwar production and trade trends, 3
Willcox, Westmore, xi
Williams, John, xi
World Development Fund, 203
World trade, *see* Trade
Wyndham White, Eric, xi